THE END AND THE BEGINNING

THE END AND THE BEGINNING

by

SISTER GILES

[signature: Sister Giles]

The Memoir Club

© Sister Giles 2007

First published in 2007 by
The Memoir Club
Stanhope Old Hall
Stanhope
Weardale
County Durham

British Library Cataloguing in
Publication Data.
A catalogue record for this book
is available from the
British Library

ISBN: 978-1-84104-170-4

Typeset by TW Typesetting, Plymouth, Devon
Printed by RPM Print & Design, Chichester

For you all, with love

List of Illustrations

Foreword

I am much honoured to commend this book. It is a unique story of an unusual person, whose life is lived for other people with humour, enjoyment and humility. To spend an hour with Sister Giles is to be cherished, understood, stimulated and amused. She finds a wavelength with all her friends, and brings a sure courage to those facing death, and reassurance to those whose lives are troublesome.

This story of how she acquired the discipline of selflessness both in Convent life and in her work outside is beautifully told and is never sanctimonious; her Faith shines through all she does, but the kind twinkle in her eye stops us, her friends, from despair at the distance we fall behind her.

Those who read this story will surely become her friends and will feel her warmth.

Iona Wake-Walker MBE, JP, DL

The Beginning

I NEVER THOUGHT TO BECOME A NUN.
I never attended a Catholic school, nor nursed a childhood infatuation for some religious sister. I was sent to a beloved prep school, walked two miles to the local parish church in crocodile each Sunday, shinned down drainpipes for a dare, and achieved three out of a hundred for arithmetic.

I had always sensed a presence of what I perceived as 'God'. My mother had Christian Scientist friends and I never forgot the printed card that hung above my bed:

Where're I am, God is,
Since this is so
No place can safer be
Than where I go.

I was close to my mother. My father had left us when I was seven, my sister barely two. We lived in Sussex. Her marriage breakdown precipitated my mother into a writing career in order to maintain us. She was successful, and I was very proud of her. Her agent would take us to lunch at Kettners on our way back to school. Once I remember meeting Agatha Christie when we were waiting in his office in Fleet Street. Owing to wartime paper shortage there were galley proofs for lavatory paper there.

I took responsibility for my sister very seriously. She was pretty and when we dressed up she made a perfect Snow White, whilst I played each of the seven dwarfs in turn. There was an element of the entertainer in my make-up. Later, I obtained a scholarship to Webber-Douglas, the school of drama in South Kensington, but I was no incipient Sarah Bernhart.

Engaged at nineteen, I was beset by guilt at breaking it off, but read a book by chance which included an essay on Thérèse of Lisieux. I telephoned the only Catholic I knew. Her name was Evelyn Ramsden and she had not long before translated Ibsen's *Peer Gynt*, which I had seen at the New Theatre.

'I think you should meet Father Francis Devas, a Jesuit Priest at Farm Street,' she suggested when I said I should like to know more about the Catholic Church. I had heard of Farm Street Church. I associated it with society weddings. I made an appointment.

'Why do you wish to become a Catholic?' Father Devas enquired.

'I'm not sure,' I replied. 'I simply feel certain that I should.'

His smile was mischievous. 'You'll never get married,' he announced. 'Every young man will go off to become a Benedictine monk at Ampleforth or Downside, and all you'll be left with is Italian waiters!'

I was received into the Catholic Church on 22 July that year. Evelyn produced champagne and suggested I stay for a while with Elizabeth and Harry Iddesleigh, friends of hers whose inherited house, Pynes, near Exeter, I later discovered had been designed by Inigo Jones. I was thrust into an atmosphere both literary and Catholic. Elizabeth was a niece of Hilaire Belloc, her mother the legendary Mrs Belloc Lowndes. I slept in the 'Disraeli' room and suspected little had changed since his day. I watched a mouse run up the bedpost, travel along the top drapery and descend the post at the pillow-end where it ran along the bolster. We dressed for dinner and shivered. Elizabeth wore lisle stockings and snow-boots beneath her velvet gown. Harry Iddesleigh and I recited Compline each evening in the chapel, and it was from Pynes that I was privately confirmed by Archbishop Grimshaw of Plymouth, who tapped me on the shoulder and said, 'Now go forth in the Holy Spirit . . .'

A few months later my mother became a Catholic, my sister not for a year or two. Lorna Wishart acted as sponsor for my mother. One of the unique Garman sisters, she was very beautiful. Yasmin, Lorna's daughter by Laurie Lee, was still a child. Only later, in Sintra, did I meet her sister Mary Campbell. Lorna died in 2000 soon after my mother, a day after her eighty-ninth birthday, and I was asked to give a 'memory' of her for a service after the funeral. My sister still has the Spanish crucifix Lorna gave my mother. I can shuffle like cards the pack of intervening years before entering the convent. I pull out a month here and there: always an adventure but never an assurance.

I met Leonard Cheshire and helped at his first home, Le Court, near Petersfield. The original house had belonged to his aunt, and his parents still lived at the lodge. Primrose, his mother, would invite me to tea on Saturdays, producing cucumber sandwiches and Earl Grey tea. When Leonard succumbed to TB we would visit him together at the sanatorium in Midhurst.

A friend asked me to help with the YMCA in Germany and I found myself in uniform and had giggles. (Yet we managed a visit to Heidelberg and the Necker valley, and motored back up the Romantischestrasse, which was lovely.) In London again, momentarily living in Devonshire Street, a friend pointed out an advertisement for a private secretary to Gerald Constable Maxwell. He lived with his wife, Carrie, in Hampshire. I typed only with two fingers, three if I concentrated, and got the job. I was given a flat at the top of the house with a view to the lake. Wagtails and nuthatches came to the parapet outside my windows. I seldom had to type but often drove the car or filled a gap for lunch or dinner parties. When Carrie's grandson, Edward, had me to a special birthday lunch at Arundel a few years ago, I vividly recalled the small bundle I was allowed to hold in those days soon after his birth. I left the Constable Maxwells just as Carrie was intent on building the chapel. I never saw it finished, but I remember James Lees Milne as a possible architect. Soon after entering the strictest of enclosed convents Carrie sent me an invitation to one of the children's wedding. My memories of the family were always affectionate.

I put down the pack. No shuffling necessary now. The next stage becomes indelible. More than an adventure, and certainly the beginning of an assurance I had been unconsciously seeking. I was about to be led in an unimaginable circle: 'Through the unknown, remembered gate,' T. S. Eliot wrote,

And the end of all our exploring
Will be to arrive where we started,
And know the place for the first time.

Amen.

Chapter 1

FOXGLOVES, HEAVY WITH PURPLE thimble flowers, towered in every hedgerow bordering the lanes. Motoring down, two swans had taken off from water meadows to our right, flapping with rhythm across the dual carriageway. It was late May.

We stopped at Simonsbath to eat. It was twenty-five years since I had entered a pub. There were dark oak settles and the walls were hung with sporting prints and trophies. The once familiar atmosphere came back to me, the smell of fresh-drawn ale, the bar conversation. I sat in the corner Julie indicated. She fetched two glasses of light beer. 'Try that!' she grinned, and consulted the tariff. We ate sausages, bacon and mushrooms. A young man stood at a fruit machine and the constant flashing distracted me. I had never seen one before. I sipped the light beer.

I glanced at my watch. One-thirty. My community would be in the chapel for the office of None. There would have been a celebration lunch because of Ascension Day, unaccustomed talking in the refectory. A glass of rhubarb wine perhaps, and a chocolate each, passed round in the box from a kind donor. The monastic 'hour' of None always followed the procession from refectory to chapel after lunch. Once, I remembered, the effects of the rhubarb wine had gone to my head.

'How far to go?' I asked Julie.

'About another hour – and the last stretch is even better! We'll see her soon.'

I'd almost forgotten that Julie, on whom I was relying for this journey, was Elizabeth's daughter. I was being transported to a destination I could scarcely imagine, yet with a curious sense of purpose that had persisted for almost a year. We walked to the parked car. It was comfortable enough in the front, but the back seats and the boot were wedged with cartons, a black plastic bin-liner, a heavy typewriter, blankets and two ancient suitcases. It looked as if I had come from the convent prepared for siege. We crossed Exmoor. Sunlight was brighter here than in Sussex. Soon we caught a glimpse

of rock cliffs to the north-west. The road began to narrow. We took
a sign for Woolacombe and soon afterwards another, to the right. The
lane began to descend. Round the corner we saw the stark edge of
the North Devon coast, a framework for the distant sea. Down and
down we went, in second gear now. The bends were almost
hairpin. Woods, newly green, swept upward on each side of the
valley, stone houses appeared to sprout from ledges. As we reached
the lower level cottages, thatched and white-rendered, huddled
closely together. Red fuchsia was everywhere. The Hollies was set in
a garden of some size. The stone house, of moderate proportions,
grew from its surroundings rather as if the house were a feature of the
landscaping, and not the other way round. There were lawns and
herbaceous borders, a disused tennis court and terraced walls from
which spilled rock plants of every kind. Pine trees stood across from
the lane, behind the inn. Rooks had their nests in these. Later I
should see buzzards over the valley, but not today. There was no one
in the house.

Julie and I unloaded the car and stacked my refugee belongings
upstairs in a room with a view to the rocky bay. I opened the sash
window. A few flies, long since dead, fluttered to the floor. Sunlight
had faded the wide, once polished, planks.

A large Victorian mahogany cupboard stood against the wall and I
caught sight of myself in the long glass. I had forgotten. Were my
Abbess to see me now! I'd made the trousers in the convent vestment
room. The pattern had been taken from a pair donated for work in
the garden. I had also made the grey anorak I wore, lined with
brushed nylon salvaged from the jumble box. For a change of clothes
there was a blue linen skirt made from a remnant found in the garret.
I liked the skirt; the colour felt right Now I combed my hair and
hoped it would pass. I'd shaped it as best I could. I'd used nail scissors,
with the back of a Vaseline tin for a glass. Twenty-five years ago it
had been dark; now it was almost white. I walked downstairs. Julie
had made a pot of tea.

'Drink this, then we'll go to the hospital,' she said. 'Basil will be
with her now. We'll get the last half-hour of visiting time.'

I wanted to pray, to feel that security of unspoken support to
which I had become accustomed, but the events of the day, the
newness, had dulled any ability to concentrate. I fingered the note
I'd received five days earlier from Elizabeth, which was in my pocket

'. . . thank you for everything, the lovely lilies of the valley, the Julian of Norwich card which keeps me going – and knowing you are nearly here. This cottage hospital where I am having these tests is really lovely . . . it is run for the patients and not for the look of the place. Consultants come from Barnstaple and one comes to see me on Monday as they don't seem to know why I have a high sediment-action rate. It is said to be an indication – but they have to find out what of! I still have a lot of pain when my head is up . . .'

Half an hour later Julie and I walked into the ward. It held six beds and Elizabeth lay on the right. It was almost eight months since I'd seen her in the convent parlour. She opened her eyes and the shock I now felt was submerged in the radiance of her remembered smile. She held out her hand.

Chapter 2

I SAT WITH MY ABBESS, trying to describe my reasons, wondering if these were genuine. Two days before, very early on a July morning, I had walked in the garden. The time was five-thirty, the loveliest part of the day. Soon we should be called to the chapel for Readings, the first 'hour' of the Church's breviary. The limes were flowering and the scent floated on the air. White summer jasmine starred the flint wall and already the bees were busy.

I'm not given to interior voices. I have never heard one. It was not a voice, as such, that I heard. It was similar to something I had felt in Assisi years before, and whatever it was then had resulted in my becoming a nun. I'd perched on a rock high above those cascading rooftops, the basilica stretched like a fortress below, hungry for the fresh Italian bread I'd carried up with the fat red grapes and bel paese cheese. The sun had been warm on my back, cowbells a stunted echo in the distance. A lizard, I remember, shared my rock, motionless, eyelids closed, sunning himself. I thought of Saint Francis. Intervening centuries were telescoped as I sensed his romantic discarding of all for Christ. Lunch half eaten, I'd had an indelible impression of that unique Franciscan calling. 'Don't say I have to become a NUN!' I'd addressed the cloudless sky. Such a possibility had never occurred to me.

Weeks later, in England again, I'd run into an elderly priest I knew. Without enthusiasm I'd asked if he considered I had a vocation. He was Irish. He had speedwell eyes and his face was as creased as a brown paper bag. 'Didn't I always know you had!' he'd smiled. 'But it should be a contemplative order, I think. Shall I write to the reverend mother I know, a good friend of mine?' Six months had passed before I'd actually entered the convent, ignorant, apprehensive. I'd walked through the great front door with no preconceived ideas bar the impact from that day in Assisi. As an enclosed nun I had found an unimagined happiness.

Two summers ago, Ambrose and Monica had brought their friend Elizabeth to visit me in the convent parlour. 'You must meet!' they'd said, which filled me with foreboding. Ambrose and Monica had done most of the talking. They spoke in unison; I thought of them as hyphenated. Elizabeth and I had sat observing one another; she'd smiled and asked if she might visit me on her own. She wore a faded cotton skirt, the same blue as her eyes. On the first of those visits she told me she had recently inherited her parents' house in North Devon. She and Basil, her retired husband, would be moving there that September. She had an indefinite notion of running The Hollies as a place of retreat, she said, somewhere to find peace, where people could come to be refreshed spiritually. This morning, I wanted to explain to my Abbess, it was as though in the bright early sunlight I'd envisaged myself there with Elizabeth, helping her. It sounded naive, the outcome of wishful thinking or a desire to escape the constrictions of religious life. Yet, as I walked in the garden, it had been almost as if I'd experienced it, as if it were already fact. What possibility, I asked my Abbess, could there be of such a mission? Had I, an enclosed nun, hope of permission to work outside the community, yet remain within its framework? Twenty-five years had passed surprisingly quickly. Noviciate days of enthusiasm – and sometimes despondency – merged to a routine of prayer and work, recreation and laughter. Bells and obedience dictated our occupations. Austerity bore no particular hardship after a time. Bare floors, a thick brown habit that almost stood up on its own, odd conventions observed over centuries, became part of a life which was strangely fulfilling. Enclosure, for me, was never claustrophobic.

But, I wrestled, was I now deceiving myself? When I entered the Order, I'd prayed. 'Give me the grace,' I'd demanded with the audacity of youth, 'to love and make present your love.' I'd always clung to that aspiration, but had not bargained for the variety of ways by which it might be accomplished. Love itself was never limited by a vow of chastity. Deprivation of physical love, I could understand, ran risks of a grasping at straws, but I had never seriously considered running away.

My Abbess listened to my attempted explanation. Papers lay scattered on her desk awaiting attention. She was largely built, her movement unhurried. She amply filled her swivel-chair. 'Wait a few months,' she said, not unkindly. 'I think this will pass.' I knew, without being told, that she suspected the menopause.

I thanked her and returned to the church vestment room. For the last eighteen months I'd been cutting out and sewing chasubles and stoles in a variety of designs and colours. The floor was littered with scraps of scarlet or green brocade.

I also made long black gowns for the ecclesiastical Knights of Malta. Two of these, half finished, hung on wooden hangers from the picture rail. White moiré silk cuffs waited to be attached to wide sleeves. On the table white fleurs-de-lis and intricate segments of the Maltese crosses lay ready to stitch to the front of the gowns. I picked up a cotton reel from where it had fallen. The vestment room was at the top of the house, part of the old wing. I walked to the window. Sister Agatha was far below attending her bees. She wore her beekeeper's veil and white overalls, a strange figure among the rhododendrons where the beehives stood. Recently there had been a swarm and she and Sister Peter had spent lunch-time up a ladder enticing the queen into a skep. There was no untoward activity today. Nearer the house Fred walked to a better patch of sun. He sniffed at a forgotten bone but it held no interest There was washing on the clothes-line by the field. Some of the 'chemises' had blown over their pegs, winding round the line. Had I been an artist I should have wanted to paint a line of washing. I turned back to the vestments.

Elizabeth wrote from North Devon. When I answered her letter I tried to describe what had happened. 'Could you look at the idea objectively?' I finished.

'I pray every day for you – and myself – to know God's will in the matter,' she replied, 'but I also fall over backwards not to influence your decision. No – to look at the idea objectively is one thing I cannot do . . .'

When Father Christopher came to see the community I asked his opinion. He was perfectly clear.

'If it is what God asks of you, then it will come about,' he said. 'My advice is that you live your present vocation faithfully and continue to pray. You will know if it is what you are meant to do.'

I tried to take his advice. Days and weeks passed. We rose at five each morning, sang psalms and hymns and recited the prayers of the Church. We sat in the refectory, tables set in the 'square horseshoe' of monastic tradition. We drank soup from our pottery bowls and wiped these with bread before receiving the following course. We spoke and laughed at recreation – and sometimes when we should

A refectory place – the pottery bowl opens in two halves; food is taken in one and bread and a tiny butter dish is kept in the other. The table napkin is blue and white check

not – and in between we worked. In summer we weeded and hoed or harvested potatoes in the field, and throughout the year there were floors to be swept, or cooking to be done, or sewing or setting up type for the printing press, always depending on whatever task we were allotted.

At Christmas Elizabeth wrote that she and Basil had gone down with influenza. I knew Basil had retired from the Royal Navy some years before, that he was older than Elizabeth. 'He has recovered quite quickly,' she told me, 'but somehow I seem to have lost a bit of substance and nothing, I'm afraid, is getting done. Apart from my physical ineffectiveness it's not altogether a bad thing,' she added. 'I was glad to miss the glitter side of Christmas, and the real peace was more than it has ever been . . .'

A pain in her neck began to trouble her. She thought she had wrenched a muscle, or even slipped a disc, and went to see an osteopath. The discomfort continued and she wrote of seeing a doctor. By Easter there was no improvement and tests were arranged. I was anxious. I wished I could dispel this with a greater faith.

A day or two later I was asked to attend a meeting at Douai Abbey. I represented the Order on a consultative committee that had been set up to advise and help contemplative communities. Kneeling in the side chapel after Mass on the final day, it seemed as if the original conviction I'd sensed last July became a clarion call. Quite suddenly, what had been indeterminate seemed tangible. It was no clear-cut plan, but an absolute inner assurance that now the door stood open. The relief I felt was immense.

Sister Ursula welcomed me on my return to the convent. Her curvature of the spine, probably caused by years of sleeping in the upright position prescribed for the Order since the fifteenth century, was severe. She looked up at me sideways, like a tortoise from beneath the load of its shell. 'Mother Abbess is in her room,' she told me. 'She will be glad to hear about your meeting. Have you had a good time?'

When I knocked at her door, the Abbess raised her head with a smile. She invited me to sit down. I described the events of the last few days and answered her questions. She was concerned and attentive. At last I found courage to bring up the subject of what had occurred in the chapel. 'Strange you should mention this now,' she said. 'Father Austin is coming tomorrow. You might like to talk with him.'

Father Austin was the priest from whom the community obtained permission for particular requests. For us he was the Bishop's representative and his word carried Episcopal weight.

'Oh thank you!' I said. 'That would be a great help.'

When I rose to leave her room I was assailed by a mixture of fear and elation.

That evening a cassette of Thomas Merton, the late Trappist monk, was played in the recreation room. I had always liked Thomas Merton; his books had meant a lot to me over the years. I was glad to listen. His American voice sounded brittle, like broken off pieces of crispbread.

'Love', I heard him say, 'is the very ground of God. It is the root of life. What all the world is dying for. They think they have it, but so often what they have is self-hate, and they can't see it. If we have been given the gift of recognising that ground of our being as LOVE, then give it to the world! Love the world! Tell them, just by being what you are . . .'

Give it to the world. That sounded right to me.

But what of my vows?

Father Austin was a Franciscan. I had never spoken to him privately. We met in the visitors' parlour. Where once the wrought-iron grille had separated guests from community, chairs were now placed casually and a bright rug made by Sister Rose lay in front of a two-barred electric fire. There were pink paper flowers in a pot on the window-sill.

Father Austin listened carefully. His brown habit did not reach his ankles, so sandalled feet protruded as he sat. He did not once interrupt, nor allude to my time of life.

'It is quite possible the Holy Spirit could work in this way,' he said. 'I suggest you apply for a year's leave of absence, which I am able to grant. This will not affect your vows. It will give you time to experiment, to sum up your reasons for wishing to extract yourself from your community.'

It sounded surgical, like an operation.

'I love the community —' I said defensively. He nodded and I felt my case had been judged. It was time to kneel for a blessing. I thanked him. Lamely I said, 'I'm very glad I needn't relinquish my vows.' There was nothing more I could say.

My Abbess, uncomprehending, bore with me. She had not expected the outcome of my interview with Father Austin. I knew I was a disappointment. I hated causing distress yet instinctively I was sure I must pursue this course. I picked up a monthly journal from the library table and read an article headed 'The Second Journey', quoted by Jack Dominian from a book by Gerald O'Collins. He wrote of this journey 'wherein we have found ourselves at last, and we are not really surprised that this is happening to us . . .' In those words there was an element of recognition.

A few days later a Chapter Meeting was held. The whole community gathered together. This happened regularly and was a time of discussion. The agenda might cover anything from matters of religious observance to a vote on the keeping of hens. Today it had been called because of me. I felt sick. The community suspected nothing because I had been asked not to tell them. The meeting opened with customary prayers, then the Abbess looked across at me. I knew every member of the seated community so well that I could have identified each from her individual bare feet. 'Sister Giles has something to tell us,' my Abbess announced without preamble, her expression inscrutable. My mouth was dry. Explanation seemed trite

as well as improbable. Words sounded staccato, like grapeshot. I tried
to be articulate and failed. Details were still sketchy and attempts to
elucidate what I wished in fact only enhanced its absence. The
pattern of the wood-block flooring, I felt, would be forever engraved
on my memory. It was as if I were at one remove from myself,
observing someone quite unconnected. I could sense the community's amazement.

I told them of Father Austin's suggestion of a year's leave of
absence. 'I do ask you to pray for me,' I concluded, 'and for Elizabeth
too. It will be an immense leap in the dark, but I feel convinced I
should take this step.' The meeting closed with a final prayer and the
community rose. We filed out in silence, the moment irrevocable.
Today there would be no more talking. Everyone tried to understand.
They were concerned and wanted to help where they could. As I
sorted, clearing the various lockers and shelves of equipment I'd used
for work or recreation, I was reminded of distant schooldays. The
atmosphere felt like an end of term.

Sister St Richard had been my novice mistress. She'd known me
since I entered the convent. A calligrapher, she illuminated with
perfect detail the parchment cards she designed. She also turned bowls
on the lathe. It was Sister St Richard who instructed me in the
traditions of the Order, encouraged me or mopped up my tears.
She had a head for heights and once I'd climbed with her out to
the gable roof below the spire to rescue an injured blackbird. Now,
from somewhere – I recalled Oscar Wilde – she found an old
Gladstone bag, packing it with items from the wood-shop, telling me
I might find them useful. She filled a discarded Sennacot tub with
screws, a former vitamin bottle with methylated spirit. She
included spare blades for the metal saw, three modelling tools, a
penknife with one blade missing. The claw hammer had seen
better days and the brass capsule containing a corkscrew had
belonged to her mother. Most precious, because I knew the extent
of her generosity, was a selection of sandpaper, two sheets of each
grade, that she used for her woodwork. She also tucked a tube of
adhesive into a corner of the bag. Possessions of this kind were
limited in the community. They were asked for infrequently, usually
as a present to mark a feast day or as a gift from a visiting relative.
Once I had asked for a coveted packet of Dragon's Blood wallflower
seeds.

Sister Giles and Sister Mary Francis (Sister St Richard) at the convent, 1982

'I think this new role for you fulfils a need,' said Sister Veronica Mary. 'You will feel restricted if you do not try it. I don't believe you will come back.'

My emotions were stretched, tight as a violin string.

'You should have warned me before the
touch of music, that it hurt so much.'

Those lines of Humbert Woolfe were copied into my commonplace book. I put together the books I should be allowed to take with me: Rilke's *Elegies*, the little book of *Un moine de l'Eglise d'Orient*, the *Revelations of Divine Love* by Julian of Norwich, and letters and poems I'd received and treasured. I wished I could have included the recordings of Bach and Vivaldi we sometimes exchanged for the usual reading in the refectory, or the Brahms and Sibelius and Schubert reserved for recreation time, when we knitted or sewed or pasted our recycled Christmas cards.

Elizabeth had accepted without question the prospect of my coming to The Hollies once she knew permission had been granted.

I'd been able to telephone and she sounded happy. 'We'll have so much to plan – and though my neck is still bad, I know it will be better once you're here.'

The unsought responsibility I was thrusting on her worried me. I knew she was unwell. If only Devon were closer. So much of my idea of The Hollies had been guesswork. I wondered how Basil would view my arrival. Was he as ready to expand The Hollies as Elizabeth maintained? How had she depicted me? Did I sound like some renegade, leaping over the wall? Uncertainties sifted painfully through my preparations.

I asked the Abbess if I might begin my leave of absence on the feast of St Barnabas, 11 June. She rocked slightly in her chair as if her back were painful. Meetings with her now were unavoidably strained. 'I suggest you go sooner,' she said, not unkindly. 'To prolong this waiting is unsettling both for you and for the community.'

The date was fixed for 25 May. I spent what time I could in the chapel. I needed that. Sunlight fell, a pool on the sanctuary floor. Starry poet's narcissi filled the altar bowls. Candles burned steadily, tulip-flamed, and the smell of wax mingled with the scent of flowers and incense. I knelt in my choir-stall, the position familiar. I tucked my feet into the folds of my long habit, cherishing the silence. Elizabeth was to enter hospital for a few days. There were to be further tests. She told me Julie could bring me down in the car on 28 May. 'That's Ascension Day,' she added. 'Lovely.'

Ambrose and Monica offered to fetch me from the convent on the Monday. To stay two nights with them, they suggested, would ease the transition from one sort of world to another. They also, I supposed, felt a certain responsibility for the unforeseen outcome of their introduction of Elizabeth. 'Ambrose will come for you at five o'clock, darling,' Monica told me on the telephone. I assembled my so-called belongings. Included were a sewing box, water colours, glass engraving tools, two blankets and the calico sheets from my bed, besides the books and garments I'd made. Sister St Richard unearthed two suitcases from the garret. One had no hinges but still retained its latch and lock, the other had only one latch and a rope for a handle. I was given a box containing offcut paper from the print room; letter paper could be expensive and the £50 in my purse might not go far. I obtained permission to take the old typewriter no one else used. I washed my gumboots. Someone produced a packet of candles and a dozen boxes of matches from the storeroom. I hoped they were stowed far enough away from the methylated spirit.

At four-thirty my Abbess, Sister St Richard, Sister Veronica Mary and I stood waiting in the hallway. Not the main entrance, but a second less used door. Words between us were superficial, those of reality already spoken. My habit was clean and pressed. There seemed to be all time and no time. I noticed my old straw garden hat aslant one of the leaning gumboots. I knew the door would not be opened until the doorbell rang.

The bell rang. Sister Veronica Mary stepped forward to open the door. Ambrose stood there smiling and eyed the stacked items. 'Ah!' he said. He greeted us, then set about stowing bags and suitcases into the boot. He placed what the boot could not hold on the back seat, with the heavy typewriter and my thick brown cloak. He took the gumboots and jokingly donned my garden hat. Perched on his balding head, it gave him the appearance of a benign garden gnome.

I knelt for a final blessing. 'Bless you, dear,' said my Abbess. Sister Veronica Mary gave me a hug. Blindly I felt for Sister St Richard's hand.

The door stood open. Without looking back I walked to the waiting car.

Monica held out her arms. She was on the doorstep waiting for us. The journey had been quite short. 'Come in, come in!' she beamed. 'Leave the unloading to Ambrose.'

Embarrassed, I did so, following her into the hall. Any hesitation I felt was overcome by her gust of laughter. She and Ambrose laughed frequently. They had played together as children, grown up with one another and, when married, the children they produced were almost replicas of themselves. Grandparents now, they expended their energies on countless good causes, always compassionate. She led me upstairs to a bedroom three times the size of my convent cell. 'We've put you in here, darling,' she stated. 'Your bathroom is this one – towels there on the hot rail – and why don't you change straight away so that you get used to your new clothes from the start?'

The decision to leave off my habit had been reached because of questions that might be asked were I to wear it when out of the enclosure for long. To be recognised as a member of the Order, yet living a wholly secular life, could lead to misunderstanding. I realised this, it was part of the cost. Monica smiled and said she would wait downstairs. The one-latch suitcase now lay upon the chaise-longue in the window bay. It was a light room, the impression sunny despite the late afternoon. A small earthenware jug held forget-me-nots, wall-flowers and an early sprig of honeysuckle. The dark tallboy on which it stood heightened their colour. The bed was enormous. I thought of my convent cell, nine feet by eleven, which held only a narrow bed, a stool, a cupboard – still referred to as a 'presse' – and the books we were permitted to keep there. This room seemed palatial.

I took off my spectacles. They were for reading, but I'd worn them continually from laziness, as removing them repeatedly was tiresome. I extracted the three black-headed pins from my veil, at a loss where to put these. Eventually I placed them in an ornamental dish beside the flower jug. Automatically I folded my black veil. A white kerchief was tied at the nape of my neck and I unloosed the tapes, pulling it over my head. My hair, still short despite encouragement, bore the semblance of a wave. I saw this in the glass. Off came my scapular, then the white cord girdle with its knots to signify the vows. Carefully I laid upon the bed the rosary which hung from it. The beads were of polished wood turned, so it was said, from an olive tree grown in the Garden of Gethsemane. I thought of the day I had received them, together with my habit.

From the cardboard suitcase I took the brown trousers I'd made. I stepped into them and hoped the cut was not too revealing. At any rate the shirt need not be tucked into the waist. I kept on my sandals. The pale carpet dulled any sound as I walked.

For a few moments I stood on the landing, an actress with stage-fright about to make an entrance. I took a deep breath and descended the stairs, as lightly as I could.

Ambrose and Monica came from the sitting room, together exclaiming at the apparition. 'You look splendid! Where are your spectacles? Turn round! Where did you get that shirt?' Excitement cut short every sentence. 'But your hair is almost white! I can't believe it! The transformation –'

Blushing, I attempted a model's pose. There was much kind-hearted banter, laughter, genuine and loving. They teased with a warmth that melted my anxieties. 'Come and drink a glass of sherry!' they commanded. I sank into a winged armchair. I needed the sherry. I crossed my legs, then uncrossed them, unsure of my role.

Much later, after dinner, Monica suggested an early night. I was still confused and a little light-headed from the wine that had followed the sherry. We'd eaten grilled sole, quite different from the frozen fish we ate in the refectory, fried and kept warm till lunch-time. After it we'd tucked into a hot meringue pudding, and Ambrose had pressed me to eat more than I needed.

I said goodnight and followed Monica upstairs. She ran my bath, pointing out a foaming essence that made the water soft. I wallowed, feeling guilty. Baths had been permitted twice weekly when I entered the convent, ten minutes allowed in the bathroom, the bath to be cleaned before leaving with the scouring powder there for the purpose; linoleum on the floor was cracked where the door had continually scuffed it. Later, in bed, I reached for my breviary on the table beside me. I read the office of Compline. In my mind's eye I saw the convent chapel, electric light extinguished, candles alone burning before the statue of Our Lady. The community, as it had done through the ages, would be singing the plainchant 'Regina Caeli', a final commendation of the day. I recalled the silence as the last echo faded, quickly turning from the memory.

I lay down, exploring the unfamiliar width of the bed with my toes. The sheets were smooth, the mattress gently sprung, a distant cry from the straw-filled mattress in my cell. I'd stuffed that myself, as we all had during noviciate. Almost convex at first, over the years it had become moulded to my form, warm as a hamster's nest. I turned off the bedside lamp. Light from outside filtered through the metal framework of the window. Somewhere, quite far off, a dog barked.

Sybil Thorndike, a friend once told me, wore her make-up for the glory of God. Observing myself in the bathroom glass it occurred to me that I might profitably do the same. The following morning I consulted Monica.

'I think that's a good idea,' she said, 'I'll see what I can find.'

At lunch-time she produced a bag from the local chemist's shop. It contained a tube of foundation cream, a compact of compressed powder and an anaemic shade of lipstick. I thanked her warmly. We applied them to my face and I was surprised how easy it was. I remembered as though it were yesterday. The result was only a slight improvement, but it helped. I should have liked to try a touch of the blue eyeshadow I admired on Monica, but felt that might be going too far. We also discussed my hair.

'I have these . . .' said Monica, as I sat before the looking glass. She threw upon the dressing-table a selection of small, bright blue plastic hair rollers. I had never come across them before. Monica demonstrated their use, attaching hairpins to secure them in place. She suggested I wind my hair round them that night. She was quite serious. I laughed and promised I'd think about it.

That afternoon we walked to the post office and I opened a savings account with my £50, because Ambrose said I should not carry the notes about. I retained £10 and felt affluent. We never handled money in the convent. The post office lady was very helpful and probably thought me mentally deficient. Ambrose did most of the negotiating. Transactions finished, we went on down to the seafront. The tide was out and there was a smell of stranded seaweed. Shingle shelved steeply and groynes extended untidily into the sea. It was calm, the tiny incoming ripples tipped with lacy foam. It was years since I'd stood at the sea's edge. Up in my bedroom that evening I did what I could with the hair rollers. They were fiendishly difficult to manage. When I got into bed and lay down, I was afraid of moving my head. The pain was excruciating. I stuck it for half an hour then propped myself up on the pillow. I was not prepared for torture, not for Sybil Thorndike, nor for Monica nor, in this case, even for the glory of God. I unwound my hair from the blue plastic rollers. Monica laughed the following morning. She said we might manage with kirby grips.

Julie, Elizabeth's daughter, was to pick me up at tea time. I'd never met her and had no idea what she knew of me. I wondered how much Elizabeth had told her, trying to imagine what I should feel in the circumstances. The morning passed swiftly. We attended Mass at the local church and I had to keep one eye on Monica because it had been so long since I'd knelt in a pew. I felt strangely exposed; the convent choir-stalls had been quite different. I prayed that I should be guided through whatever the coming year might hold. Words from the Epistle to the Philippians came into my head: 'I can do all things through Christ which strengtheneth me.' That verse had comforted me often. I knew I had to hold on to it now. Afterwards we walked home to breakfast and Ambrose made coffee which pervaded the house with its delicious smell.

I hardly knew how to thank Ambrose and Monica. They had gone out of their way to help over these past two days. During the morning they told me always to count on them should any need arise and I knew that I could. My first glimpse of them, years before, had been an example of their kindness. They'd brought news of my godmother, whom they had met when she stayed in the village. She had fallen ill and they had found her a nursing home, visiting her daily whilst she was there. They had taken her flowers and later, on her death, attended the funeral. Since then they'd come at regular intervals to see me in the convent parlour. Sometimes I was requested to tone down the noise when Ambrose told stories and Monica laughingly capped them. I wondered if they ever spoke seriously, even to themselves. They brought bags of glacier mints which we sucked throughout the visit.

When Julie drew up in the car she had her children with her. Two of them tumbled out leaving Julie to unstrap the baby. Ambrose introduced us. Dark hair framing her bright round face, she bore no resemblance to Elizabeth. The children drank fruit juice and answered questions without elaborating. Like a magician, Ambrose produced small sweets. Monica cut slices of Swiss roll and I remembered the trayload of these the community had been sent once from Marks & Spencer. They had passed their sale date and we'd each been handed an entire Swiss roll, peeling the cellophane off and consuming them as if they were bananas.

We transferred my luggage from the garage. The typewriter and all but one suitcase had been stacked there when Ambrose unloaded his car. Julie's estate was considerably larger. I was to stay the night at the farm in Hampshire and found myself dreading this. The journey had to be broken because the children were not coming to Devon and had to be taken to school before we left in the morning.

At last the moment came to leave. Ambrose and Monica hugged me as if I were one of the children. For a second I wished there were not the need for a further parting, that I might remain longer within their structured life which ran so predictably. As we moved off they stood together, waving, until we turned the corner. Julie, beside me at the wheel, chatted easily. Every now and then she lifted her voice to admonish the children. 'Stop it, both of you!' she shouted. The baby was strapped into a child's seat between the other two. They bickered a great deal, their small voices a half-heard accompaniment to our conversation. I had the sensation of being one step further

upon a predestined journey. Tomorrow we should head for the West
Country. It would be Ascension Day.

We were tired. Basil had returned from the cottage hospital. He was
nodding, seated in a faded armchair beside the unlit fire. An ornate
gilt clock stood upon the marble chimneypiece. By now it was after
six. Basil rose from his chair, greeting Julie, who then introduced me.
She was his step-daughter; he and Elizabeth had no children of their
own. Elizabeth had married him, much older than herself, when
widowed and left with two young children soon after the war.

Kate, the red setter, lay by the open French door. Basil offered us
drinks. His hair, now receded, was still dark though his complexion
was grey. The pockets of his tweed jacket bulged, so did his waistline.
He poured us sherry and helped himself to whisky from a carved oak
court cupboard. He was clearly worried about Elizabeth, yet I had
the impression he was relieved I had come. Elizabeth had spoken
little of Basil. It seemed unaccountable that we had not previously
met. Julie flopped on to an armchair. She spoke of the children,

Elizabeth with a grandchild

relating amusing incidents, telling of what they had said. Basil listened politely, but Julie's descriptions obviously failed to register. He reached for his drink, as if that were his contact with reality. I asked his opinion of Elizabeth's illness.

'Hope she'll be back soon,' he said, putting down his tumbler on the table at his elbow.

I asked if he'd had a report from the hospital. 'Probably not till tomorrow,' he smiled, though I felt he was trying to reassure himself rather than me. Seeing her lying flat on the hospital bed just now, I'd wondered if Elizabeth had contracted some severe form of arthritis. She had lost weight and looked frail, her face appeared angular, her cheeks hollowed. Blood tests had revealed the high sedimentation rate she'd mentioned in her note; analgesics seemed of little avail.

'Very glad you've come,' Basil smiled at me. 'Elizabeth will be pleased too. Let me get you a drink.'

I wondered if his memory were more impaired than I'd realised. He struck me as disorientated, protecting himself with an imagined life as he wished it to be. Then I chided myself. With his wife so unwell, he had every reason to be preoccupied. Julie turned to me, stretching an arm towards Kate.

'Come on!' she said. 'We'll take Kate for a run. I'll show you the bay and we'll call in to Nell on the way back. You must meet Nell, we've known her since we were children.'

Before leaving we put a shepherd's pie in the oven, which Julie had made early that morning. Basil looked up at her with sudden mock severity. 'Is it a shepherd's pie or a cottage pie?' he enquired. 'Do you know the difference?' Julie did, but I did not – we never ate meat in the convent.

'Well, I'm glad,' he said as she passed the test. 'I prefer that.' We left him with another glass of whisky.

Julie slipped Kate's leash. The dog raced away, chestnut hair streaming, sure of her ground. Julie talked easily. We had travelled a long way since this morning. The car's capsule environment promoted confidence; she'd been eager to speak of her life and family. My head teamed with impressions.

We were too exhausted to walk far over the boulders on the beach. Any exploring of the countless rocky pools was left to another day. Kate, reluctantly, returned when Julie called and we made our way back to the sea wall. Nell's house, white-rendered, stood high up from the lane. Across the driveway a washing line drooped from a tall pole to a fixture on an adjacent outbuilding. We ducked beneath this to reach the gate. The front porch opened on to a paved courtyard, bright with tubs of flowers. The low wall bordering this was untidy with large shells and flowerpots. A wire container holding bird nuts hung from a pergola near the gate.

Nell came through the porch and Kate wagged her feathered tail, her slim body swinging from the impetus. A small black poodle followed at Nell's heels, barking at the intrusion.

'How are you, darling?' Nell greeted Julie as she eyed me.

Julie once more made introductions. Nell invited us into the house and we followed her down two steps to the sitting room. The room was low-ceilinged; the casement window at the far end overlooked the distant bay. I was struck by two brass lampstands beside the fireside chairs. They were in the form of rearing cobras.

As Basil had done, Nell insisted we take a drink with her. I sipped my second sherry. Nell spoke with Julie, interested enquiries about the children, references to members of the family about whom I knew so little.

'How do you find Basil?' she asked.

'Bit repetitive!'

Julie smiled. 'How is he coping with Ma's being away?'

Nell's reply echoed Basil. 'Oh, she'll be back soon,' she said, dismissing any other possibility. 'Basil was worried in case you might not want to come,' she added, turning to me.

My attention had wandered as Nell and Julie talked. There were photographs on most available surfaces about the room. Family groups, weddings, children as well as animals posed with fixed expression from every sort of frame. I tried to imagine who they were. Then I thought of the community. They would be at recreation now, perched upon low rush-seated stools, knitting or contrasting coloured silks for their embroidery, while they exchanged conversation or read aloud snippets of news from family letters. I wondered if there'd been another swarm for Sister Agatha. Nell's last remark brought me to heel.

'I've come!' I assured her, 'and I want to be of any use I can – though you'll have to advise me.'

'I believe you're a Roman Catholic?' Nell enquired.

I was aware of my home-made trousers and could have done with my long brown habit.

'I shall be going to Ilfracombe on Sunday,' she said. 'I can take you to your church and go on to mine. I expect you'd like that?'

I was grateful. I knew there was no Catholic church in the village. I thanked her, thinking how capable she looked. Her figure, ample yet with a certain elegance, emanated strength of character. She wore ear-rings and an enamelled brooch was pinned to her lilac jersey dress. In her seventies, I imagined, as I looked at her across the darkening room. Her eyes had a penetrating quality, even behind her spectacles. Her softly waved grey hair was secured in a knot. I felt quite certain I should sit in this room again.

We declined a further sherry. 'Basil will be waiting for his shepherd's pie,' said Julie. I felt her tone suggested duty rather than affection, as if she were accustomed to discussing him with Nell. 'We'd better go.' We said goodnight and Nell came to her courtyard to see us off. 'See you soon, dear!' she called to me.

Julie was to return to Hampshire the following day. Before she left she said she would take me to the cottage hospital, with a brief inspection of the town first. We left The Hollies at eleven and drove the few miles to the town. The descent to the harbour was steep. We stopped at traffic lights and Julie pointed out a tall figure striding down the hill. 'That's Peter!' she smiled. 'You'll meet him, he lives in the village. His grandmother was my great-aunt or something. He writes music.'

The lights turned to yellow, then quickly green. Peter had not seen us. Julie negotiated the car though narrow twisting streets. The town was thronged with shoppers, but eventually we managed to park. Young children, reluctantly clutched by overladen mothers, whined or sucked ices as we made our way towards the supermarket. It was the first I'd entered. I was amazed at the crowded shelves, the metal baskets and trolleys. The last time I had bought groceries was at the local village shop twenty-five years before. It had been a place of gossip, where you waited whilst Mr Lewes measured or weighed or cut. I recalled the smell at once: bacon, polish, paraffin, peardrops, together with an indistinguishable mixture of essential items the general stores provided. It was a long time since I had helped myself. In the community we received what we were given. Julie bought grapes for Elizabeth.

I waited outside the little ward whilst she went in to see her mother. Muted conversation filtered through half-closed doors. The corridor had an air of friendliness about it, but no one came past. Sunlight shone through an open window opposite. I had known that Julie would leave after visiting Elizabeth, yet when she came from the ward I was assailed by a sudden fear of her departure. Her confidence and brisk assurance had transmitted itself and I'd come to lean on her. Now the swift awareness of my responsibility felt overwhelming. Elizabeth had appeared so ill. How, I thought, shall I ever look after Basil? I knew nothing about him. I'd known boys in my youth, but visiting priests in the convent parlour scarcely afforded familiarity or prepared me for this.

I accompanied Julie to the car. 'You'll be all right!' she smiled. 'Glad you're here! Nell will help, she's good with Basil! I'll ring you to see how Ma gets on.' She gave me a bear-hug before opening the door. Just for a moment I wondered if she knew more of Elizabeth's illness than she quite admitted. She was eager to leave, I sensed. Perhaps she feared I should change my mind about staying. She fastened her safety belt and started the engine. Her hand was on the brake. She let in the clutch and pulled away, waving from the open window. I waved back, brightly as I could, but my diaphragm felt constricted, solid, like bread pudding. I watched until she was out of sight.

Back in the hospital, I stayed half an hour with Elizabeth. She held my hand like a child and with the other reached out to touch my hair. She hadn't seen it before because of the kerchief and veil I wore. 'It's nice!' she smiled. Then she looked at me very directly. Her eyes were astonishingly blue.

'I don't know what this thing is,' she said, 'but the pain is incessant. I want to get better. You've come, and we've so much to do.' She became practical. 'There's a house purse in my desk. You are to use this for everything. Basil will maintain it. Promise me to do this.'

Unaware of what to say, I nodded. I now realised my £50 would go nowhere. Originally I'd thought to supplement my finances by continuing to engrave glass in any spare time. Years ago I'd been lent *Initials in the Heart* by Lawrence Whistler and had written to him, asking if he thought such a craft compatible with community life. He had encouraged me, and much later I'd engraved glass for the chapel windows. Perhaps in due course there would be further opportunity.

Elizabeth continued to hold my hand. 'I feel we've been travelling towards this moment for years,' she said.

For me it was more a feeling of apprehension. Her unexpected frailty contributed to my anxiety. I longed to see her as I'd remembered her in Sussex. She looked tired. I offered her a grape. She took only one. I left after a while, taking with me a list of things to bring next time. On Monday she should have an answer to her tests and the Barnstaple consultant would come. As I looked back from the doorway I saw her eyes close.

The sun was shining although a light breeze blew sporadic clouds from the south. I had told Basil I'd try walking back the three miles over the cliff top. I could smell the sea. Climbing the lane from the town I realised how out of practice I was. My calf muscles ached.

The sun was warm, the stony path sheltered here by tall banks. I thought of Saint Francis, thankful he had founded my Order all those centuries before. It was good to walk, to have time, to notice movement in the hedgerow. I prayed. Feeling at one with my surroundings I regained a shred of peace. At the top a wooden gate opened to a rough bridle path. On impulse I climbed the gate and jumped down on to short turf. Small wild flowers starred the grass. I tried to recall their names but had forgotten. Primroses were over, their leaves yellowing. Gorse bushes leaned to the very edge of the cliff and, many feet below, I caught sight of the sea where it thrashed the base of huge rocks. I did not walk fast. Every moment needed to be stored. I remembered a phrase from Katherine Mansfield's journal: 'My mind was just like a squirrel. I gathered and gathered, and hid away.' At one point the track led close to a sheer drop and I had a moment of vertigo. I dared look nowhere but straight ahead, then the track turned inward and the fear passed. There were sheep grazing. They scattered as I approached and stood gawping on matchstick legs.

Back in the valley I tramped up the lane to The Hollies. I was tired, yet the air on the high cliff top had been exhilarating. Nell was tending the geraniums in her courtyard as I passed. She saw me and came to the stone parapet.

'How are you?' she called. 'How's Elizabeth today?'

I told her of my visit, of the walk back from the hospital. Something about her reminded me of the community. I might have been recounting an expedition to Sister St Richard. She felt like an ally, wanting to help.

'I'll go in myself soon,' she said. 'Tell Basil I'll be up to see him at six. Glad you walked over the links. Let me know if there's anything you need.' Her black poodle barked as a telephone rang in the house. Nell shouted at the dog to be quiet. ' 'Bye, dear,' she finished, turning towards the porch. I continued on my way up the lane.

Basil did not drive. He relied on Nell or other friends to take him to Elizabeth. I suspected he'd long settled into a routine that excluded more than limited decisions. The daily lunch, Julie told me, he ate at the inn; the news of the village he received in the easy atmosphere of the bar constituted safe boundaries. Elizabeth's illness, I felt, was beyond them. When I came in he was dozing over *The Times*. I greeted him and gave messages from Elizabeth. He removed his spectacles.

'Can I get you a drink?' he asked. It was becoming a refrain. I declined and felt I disappointed him. It was almost three o'clock.

'I think I need something to eat!' I explained. The walk had left me hungry. Basil smiled wistfully, put on his spectacles, and lifted his paper again.

The kitchen was approached through a scullery and contained the only sink. The sink, of shallow glazed stoneware, had been unchanged since its original installation. On either side long ridged wooden draining boards ran down to it. To the left a tall plate rack, also of wood, held plates which had been left there since Elizabeth washed them. Several others remained unwashed in the sink from last night's supper. The only modern appliance was a washing machine, about which I knew nothing. This was housed by the back door. A curious assortment of hosepipes attached it to brass taps over the sink. Unlike the scullery, the kitchen itself was light. There was a sizeable electric cooking stove. A boiler for the central heating replaced what had once been a black kitchen range; the shelf above held a variety of earthenware and pottery jugs. A scrubbed kitchen table stood in the centre of the room, its surface littered with papers, empty egg boxes, a silver bowl containing sugar, as well as a handleless cup holding a few dead wild flowers. Windsor chairs were drawn up to the table. Tops of low surrounding cupboards by the dresser were stacked with cake tins and a medley of utensils. In the corner a pile of washed but un-ironed laundry awaited attention.

I tried to recall whether I'd noticed a bread bin. I found a box actually containing eggs and knew I should probably discover butter and milk in the refrigerator. The handle of its door was damaged, but I had no difficulty in opening it. As I did so, I felt a nudge against my thigh. Kate had followed me from the sitting room. 'Hello,' I whispered, 'got the same idea?'

I telephoned the community later. I spoke to my Abbess and begged everyone to pray for Elizabeth. I knew they would. I remembered how often people asked for prayers. Notices of their requests were pinned to a board outside the chapel. It was always heartening to receive the frequent letters referring to answered prayer. I should like to have prolonged the call but was inhibited because of the cost. I sent my love and said I was fine.

Basil and I spent the early part of the evening talking together. He seemed pleased to have a companion. Nell came but left after only one drink because she had to attend a village meeting. I made my sherry last. 'Glad they let you out,' Basil confided. 'Don't like all those bars, you know.' He made it sound like prison.

I laughed, explaining that the bars were to keep people out, not in, but he remained unconvinced. 'Don't you go back,' he remonstrated.

The telephone rang in the hall. I answered it. 'I'm a friend of Elizabeth!' came a female voice. 'I'm dying to meet you! I'll be down in ten minutes . . .'

I returned to Basil. 'Who was that?' I asked him, describing the conversation.

'Avril,' he said flatly. 'What does she want?' Then he added, 'She and Elizabeth walk together.'

Unspoken words were clear from his expression.

In no time at all we heard her at the scullery door.

'Coo-ee! Here I am!' she called, limping through to where we sat in the sitting room.

She drank gin and tonic, her affected leg tucked neatly behind her good one. I guessed she'd had polio in her youth.

'Elizabeth and I have lovely walks together,' she beamed. 'She's talked so much about you. She's been simply longing for you to come. Let's hope she'll soon be home again so you can start your lovely plans for The Hollies.'

I felt at a disadvantage. Clearly she wanted to assert her prior claim on Elizabeth and I had little desire to oppose her. Basil had nothing much to say. I learned that she worked for the summer at a caravan park so had limited free time during the season. Ashamed of myself, I felt grateful.

Basil thought she had better stay for dinner. I'd earmarked a ready-made lasagne which Nell had produced, but there was only enough for two. Avril accompanied me to the kitchen and told me where to find the freezer. It stood in a room behind the kitchen, just discernible amongst furniture stacked there after the move six months before. We pushed our way past chests on which stood oil lamps, half painted canvasses, dusty crockery and many stacked books. Half-open drawers revealed oil-painting materials, fishing tackle and, strangely, an assortment of what looked like Basil's socks. The deep-freeze was very well stocked and Avril pounced on sausages.

'Just the thing!' she said brightly. 'Now for some oven chips and peas to go with it!'

She helped me cook these and we put the plates on trays which we carried to the sitting room. Basil woke up. 'That looks delicious!' he said, blinking. We ate with the tray on our knees. Kate sat with rapt attention. 'She's not allowed scraps,' Basil rebuked, as Avril slipped a morsel from her plate. After ice-cream, also from the freezer, Avril made instant coffee. She smoked a cigarette and looked satisfied.

'So glad I popped down,' she said. 'I knew Elizabeth would have wanted me to help you feel at home.' At ten-thirty she said she must be getting back. 'Don't want to get the sack!' she laughed. She said goodnight to Basil, bending to give him a kiss. I saw her to the scullery door. As she limped down the path to the car in the lane below, she waved over her shoulder. 'We'll have lots of lovely walks *à trois* in the autumn!' she called. I whistled for Kate. She had taken the opportunity to spend a penny and was round by the hydrangeas.

Chapter 3

O N MONDAY THE CONSULTANT ADVISED transferring Elizabeth to the county hospital.

A more comprehensive investigation could take place there, he said. She would be moved to Barnstaple by ambulance the following Thursday.

Throughout the Thursday it rained incessantly. The stream splashed in full spate, water dripped from every heavy branch, even the rain appeared green. I took Kate for a walk which we both disliked. Basil's anxiety affected his bowels. We rang the hospital and it was at least a relief to learn that Elizabeth had arrived there without mishap. Nell said she would drive me the fifteen miles to see her the next day.

Basil recoiled from the thought of an unfamiliar hospital. 'You go,' he encouraged me. 'I'll stay here in case Julie rings.' It was a lame excuse, but I did not tax him.

When Nell and I reached the hospital we found Elizabeth in a small ward on the first floor. Obviously sedated, she was lucid and very pleased to see us. She watched as I filled a jar with water for the rockery flowers I'd salvaged from yesterday's rain, admiring and inspecting them closely. When Nell left us after a few minutes, she turned to me, looking serious. 'Whatever the outcome of all this,' she said slowly, 'I want you to know how thankful I am that you're here. I should never have managed alone . . .'

If only I could heal her, I thought. Here and now, like the apostles.

Nell returned and we said goodbye, not wishing to tire her. Elizabeth was reluctant to release my hand. I hated leaving her. As we walked to the lift Nell whispered to me, 'I don't like the look of this.' Nor did I.

Rain still fell lightly as we drove home. 'We need cheering,' said Nell. 'We'll visit the flower festival.' I was unenthusiastic, but did not say so. We reached the cliff-top village, parking by the church in which it was being held. The scent of lilies and other arranged flowers assailed us as soon as we reached the porch.

Visitors thronged the aisles, snatches of tinned music invaded muted conversations. As we made our way round the decorated church I noticed a particular display, in honour of the Selwyn Image Screen, and could hardly believe my eyes. Selwyn Image had been a cousin of my grandmother, a Slade professor of art at Oxford in the early part of the century. The entire chancel arch was adorned by his mosaic design. Standing before it I felt a surge of consolation at finding someone remotely connected. Silently I saluted him. Nell was impressed.

'There dear!' she beamed. 'I knew we should have come!'

It wasn't till the following day that Dr Hughes called at The Hollies. He came just before lunch. He practised locally and Elizabeth and Basil were his patients.

Declining Basil's offered drink, he sat down looking grave.

'Basil,' – he spoke with kindness – 'this is going to come as a shock.' He looked across to me, also with concern. 'I'll come straight to the point. I have to tell you, as you may have guessed, that Elizabeth has cancer.' I suppose I'd known. I looked at Basil. His expression was blank, uncomprehending.

'There's a possibility they might take her to Exeter for treatment.' He turned again to me. 'Do you drive?'

'Not now,' I answered. 'My licence lapsed several years after I entered the convent. I'd have to re-take a test.'

'Then I think you should seriously consider doing so,' Doctor Hughes continued. 'Exeter is fifty miles from here. Now Basil,' he went on, 'I think you'd better get in to Barnstaple and see Elizabeth as soon as you can. She's very ill.' He might have been speaking to a child.

Basil was finding it impossible to assimilate the situation. His eyes filled with tears. Dr Hughes rose to leave. He was a large man. I took him to the door where he stood outside on the stone path. Turning to me he said, 'This is hard for you. I know how much Elizabeth counted on your coming. She told me of her plans for The Hollies and I encouraged her.' He looked back at the house. 'I'm almost more worried about Basil,' he confided. 'The shock of this, you know, could kill him, he's far from well himself. Thank God you're here. Should anything worry you, don't hesitate to let me know.'

He shook my hand and was gone. I felt cold, and utterly inadequate, but at least the rain had stopped.

Basil had remained in his chair, ashen and in tears. I knelt beside him, doing my best to comfort. He repeated Elizabeth's name again and again. At last he turned to me with a ghost of a smile. He blew his nose. 'Well, thank God you're here!' he whispered brokenly, just as Doctor Hughes had done half an hour before. That was the moment when, with swift clarity, I had an inkling of why I had come. Had I arrived on 11 June as I'd originally requested, I should have been too late. My Abbess suggested the earlier day. By 28 May I was here, the outcome of an inner compulsion that had not let me rest. Ultimately, it was also under obedience. Numb with apprehension, fearful at what was being asked of me, I prayed for strength and all the faith I needed.

Basil and I took a taxi to the hospital. This time Elizabeth was virtually unconscious, heavily sedated. Conversation was out of the question. A houseman approached us, explaining that she was too ill for treatment, that the elimination of pain was the only course left open. I told him briefly of the community from which I'd come, of a belief in prayer. He smiled sadly. 'Go on believing,' he said gently, 'but I think it will be only a matter of days.' Basil, bewildered, had not opened his mouth. After a few minutes by her bed we left Elizabeth, deep in the labyrinth of her painkillers.

Tomorrow would be the feast of Pentecost, commemorating the descent of the Holy Spirit. I read the sequence from the liturgy, ages old. 'Give them comfort when they die, give them life with Thee on high, give them joys which never end.' At two in the morning I woke abruptly, feeling a sense of release, almost euphoria. Elizabeth has died, I thought. I lay thinking of her, praying for her, praying for Basil and the children. I expected the telephone to ring. At seven I rang the hospital and got the night sister, still on duty.

'We thought she'd gone in the night,' she told me, 'but she's rallied. She's just a little stronger now.' During the morning a staff-nurse rang. 'She's asking for you,' she said, 'do you think you could possibly come?'

Basil was glad I should go. He told me he was expecting Peter to call; they were lunching together at the inn. I knew that this was his shield, that behind its protection he could pretend nothing had changed. I walked round to Mrs Coombes who lived close by. Her son was staying, and had a car. ' 'Course he'll take you,' she agreed, 'just you hop round, you'll be there in no time.' Her soft West Country voice was comfortable, like a sunny Devon lane.

Within an hour I was beside Elizabeth. A constant infusion was being administered through a syringe strapped to her chest. She was talkative but quite incoherent. The ward sister called me aside. 'Is she a Roman Catholic?' she asked. 'She keeps speaking of seeing a priest.' I suggested she get the Anglican vicar Elizabeth knew so well.

Michael came as soon as his Sunday service was over. He wore his cassock still. He brought Janet, his wife. They stood close to the bed, trying to make sense of Elizabeth's ramblings. Nick, Elizabeth's son, arrived, summoned the evening before by Basil. Julie walked in soon after. Everyone wanted to contribute, to help restore normality. Elizabeth remained confused and flushed. The atmosphere was tense. I longed for them all to leave, to stop their talking so that she might rest. A poem, written for quite another occasion, flashed into my head:

This business of dying:
I've seen it. Nothing fine about it,
Watching the person you love
Sliding into what looks like oblivion.
All those allusions to trees
Losing their leaves
And an atmosphere of autumn and decay
Giving way to the rebirth of spring –
Lovely, if you can take it.
What I need is faith:
I need Jesus, here, now,
Crying from the cross
'My God, my God, why hast thou forsaken me?'
And then, only after that,
Having seen his desolation
And knowing what came after,
Shall I be ready to say
'Yes, yes, I believe in the resurrection.'

Today was Gethsemane. Nothing fine about it. Pain had the upper hand, emotions were all but run dry. Nick and Julie, understandably distressed, hoped the agony would not be prolonged. No one expected to see Elizabeth alive the next day.

That evening we were all exaggeratedly polite. Food had to be cooked, sheets found for the beds. Wherever we went we got in each other's way. Unwashed dishes accumulated again in the scullery sink. Basil, trying to help, said he would feed Kate. Julie went off to find Peter. Suddenly homesick, I longed for my silent convent cell.

Chapter 4

ELIZABETH SURVIVED THE NIGHT.

At ten o'clock the next morning Nick dropped me off at the parish church near the hospital. I still felt numb. The familiar words of the Mass seemed remote, as if I heard them through opaque glass. By the time I reached the ward Elizabeth was restless, but still alive.

Nick was pleased to see me. He smiled as I entered the room, stooping to pick up his jacket before rising from the blue plastic chair. 'Think I'll go off for a bit,' he said. 'She seems a bit quieter now. I'll run back to the house and return this afternoon, if that's all right for you?'

I took his place on the chair. The syringe giving the infusion was still in place; nurses came frequently to check it. They were friendly, intrigued by what they had gleaned of my background. 'She's a nun,' I heard one tell another. They wanted to know why I was there, so I told them of our idea for The Hollies. 'We want it to be opened as a place of prayer or quiet spiritual renewal,' I explained.

'Oh, we must get her better!' they said with enthusiasm.'That's just the incentive she needs to win through this battle.'

Remaining there, thinking, trying to pray, it occurred to me that were a priest to read the rite of Extreme Unction in Elizabeth's presence, this might bring a measure of peace. I knew from experience the benediction it bestowed. Many times in the community I'd seen the rite administered and the relief that followed.

I did not, however, wish to impose my Catholic belief, nor was I sure such a move feasible. I asked the ward sister's opinion. She was in favour. Father Nolan, the Catholic hospital chaplain, came promptly after receiving our call. He was also the local curate, tall, good-looking, professionally attentive. 'Has she expressed a desire to be received into the Church?' he enquired. Before I could answer, Elizabeth, suddenly distinct, replied from the bed, 'Yes, I have – but – isn't God present everywhere?'

I opened my mouth to enlarge on this, but shut it again, at a loss. This precept, for her, was evidence enough. I'd heard her views on the subject many times in the convent parlour. It was not, though, the sentiment associated with a prospective convert. Instead I told Father Nolan my reason for calling him, of my immediate desire to bring Elizabeth peace. I also filled in the manner of my leave of absence from the community. He listened, nodding appropriately, as if I were confessing my sins. Eventually he picked up his stole from where he had placed it on the table. He smiled kindly in Elizabeth's direction.

'I think,' he said, 'in the circumstances, I'd best give Elizabeth a blessing.' He accentuated her name to be certain she heard. 'Please call me if she wants to see me again.' He gave the blessing, praying she should find peace. A moment later, duty completed, he was on his way.

Peter came to fetch me that evening. Nick and Julie had dropped in during the afternoon but returned to The Hollies later. Since that first glimpse at the traffic lights I had seen Peter only once. He'd come through the scullery door, ducking to pass the low lintel. Now he strode towards me across the expanse of carpet which covered the hospital foyer. 'How is she?' he asked quietly.

Truthfully I was able to tell him, 'I believe a little better.'

'Do you think I might see her a moment?'

I led him back to the ward and waited outside by the lift. He stayed only a few minutes.

Peter had come in Elizabeth's Volkswagen Beetle. As we left the hospital grounds I recounted the day's events. He knew Father Nolan. He himself was a Catholic, educated at Downside. His grandmother, a convert, had been Elizabeth's favourite aunt. 'She had a house in Devonshire Street,' he told me. 'Elizabeth always stayed with her for dances.'

In London, years before, I too had lived in Devonshire Street.

'What number?' Peter asked immediately.

I told him and sensed his amazement. 'That was my grandmother's house!' he said. 'Does Elizabeth know you were there?'

'Never thought of telling her!' I replied, as we approached the roundabout where we turned off. 'I will if there's a chance . . .'

Elizabeth showed signs of improvement. Almost imperceptibly the crisis lessened. Nick and Julie thought they should return to their families, to be recalled at once if required. I quite lost count of time. Days passed in a routine of preparation at The Hollies, followed by long hours in the hospital. Nell or Peter saw to my transport.

Basil rarely made the journey to see Elizabeth, nor did his absence seem to worry her. I began to suspect that an inability to face the prospect of her loss was part of a deeper ailment, unlikely to be resolved. It saddened me to realise that for too long their lives had been separately packed, held together by Elizabeth's Christian belief and the strength of Basil's dependence. For him, to see her ill was unbearable.

One morning the staff nurse removed the syringe drip. This was a turning point. She encouraged Elizabeth to take liquid food, asking me to feed her. We laughed as I held each spoon to her mouth like a baby. One day she was so much better that she demanded, of all things, a glass of stout. With obvious relish she even managed a joke. 'It's good for you!' she grinned.

I reported all this to Basil when I reached home. We would eat the meal I had prepared before I left, spending what remained of the evening in random conversation. Sometimes he would show me old photographs of ships he had commanded, and even older ones of his forebears. Kate would stretch out on the floor beside me, adapting to a new regime.

I wished there had been opportunity for Elizabeth to show me the kitchen. Basil knew nothing. Preparation of meals was a search for ingredients stored haphazardly in cupboards. Some had been there from her parents' time, some from much further back. The cooking scales did not work, yet a new omelette pan bore a notice 'please never wash'. I guessed how difficult she must have found the move from Sussex six months earlier. Never easy, I reminded myself, it must have been heroic in the shadow of her gathering illness.

I wrote to Father Ian Petit, the Benedictine monk who had given our community retreat last year. I asked him to pray for Elizabeth, and for me. He wrote back: 'If you get a chance to lay your hands on her and pray, then do. Do not ask me what to say, there are no rules, just be "Jesus" to her. I shall also keep her in my prayers, but it is not we who do things, it is the Lord.' Other friends too were continuing to pray. Groups in Sussex long-known to Elizabeth wrote with concern. Martin Israel, whose writing we both knew and whom Elizabeth had met, also prayed for her. After a while, the doctor reduced the painkillers.

Relatives came to visit. Elizabeth's cousin Paul, an Anglican bishop, brought his wife. These were bright summer days, when flowers and pot plants wilted.

One afternoon Avril arrived. She brought strawberries. 'We can't let the summer go without a strawberry tea!' she said brightly.

I left them to enjoy it together. No need, I kidded myself, to be *à trois* yet. As I closed the door Elizabeth reached out her hand. 'How sweet of you,' she smiled at Avril, 'but you'll have to eat some of them for me.'

Nurses came to talk, encouraged by Elizabeth's ready smile. Other patients, passing the little annexe, stopped to have a word. She had now been told she had cancer. She wanted to fight it. Paradoxically she also accepted it. We spoke of the illness openly.

'If I'm going to die, don't you see it will still be all right? I'll continue to work with you! The spirit is the enduring reality – you said it yourself!'

I remembered. I'd written from the convent that the continuity of life was never ended by death. Physical senses were no more, but the created centre of our being was eternally rooted in God. 'Nothing shall separate us from the love of God,' I'd quoted from Saint Paul. God was love, and genuine love, human in its manifestation, stemmed always from that infinite source. Elizabeth and I had hoped to impart this to those who might come to The Hollies.

We spoke of future plans for the house. Elizabeth wanted to redesign the kitchen.

We studied advertisements in the glossy pages of journals. 'We won't be slaves to their plans,' she stated, 'it has to be OUR kitchen!' I was silently thankful to think of an updated kitchen for The Hollies. She asked if she might be allowed home, but the nursing officer who came to see her thought this unrealistic. The special bed on which she was being nursed would never transfer to The Hollies. Elizabeth at once begged to be nursed on a normal bed. She was promised a review of her situation in about a week.

Chapter 5

NELL WAS EMPHATIC. 'You must take a day off,' she told me as we drove home from the hospital. I saw the sense of this but was hesitant. It was easy to feel indispensable. Nell wasn't deflected. 'You'll crack if you don't,' she threatened. After more persuasion, I agreed.

'All right,' I said, 'I'll see if I can arrange a day.'

One morning the following week, I left Basil as usual and made my way down the lane. Nell was waiting for me.

'There you are, dear!' she called. She gave me instructions. 'Take this rucksack,' she said. 'Walk over the cliff top and don't come back till this evening.'

I smiled. I knew she was right. I humped the small rucksack over my shoulders. 'You're a bully, but I'm giving in gracefully!' I laughed. 'Thank you for whatever you've packed in here.' Nell waved me off.

I set out, trying to erase thoughts of the hospital. The lane rose one-in-three as I left the village. I saw Peter's boat drawn up in its ramp as I passed his house. Not far beyond I spotted the wicket gate which Nell had told me about. Opening it I walked through to a grassy slope. When I reached the top a dramatic line of gorse-topped cliffs almost made me exclaim aloud. Sunlight picked out the graded colour of each bold escarpment, huge rocks serrated the sandy cove below. The sea, beyond the shadows, was aquamarine. I watched a small boat in the distance make its steady course.

Breath regained, I discovered a descending route towards a rocky inlet. The steeply twisting path was precipitous to my unaccustomed feet. Once down I came to a little wooden bridge which crossed great boulders, constantly lashed by the sea. The far side towered above me towards another summit. As I leaned against the bridge I noticed sea-thrift growing in tiny crevices. Nearby a pool had formed, a refuge for crabs and the coral sea anemones anchored against its wall. I'd caught a lobster further round this coast one childhood holiday. I summoned strength for the climb ahead, determined to gain the top. By the time I'd reached it I decided I'd come far enough, gratefully collapsing on to a protruding rock. I removed Nell's rucksack, using it as a pillow. Acutely aware of a sudden gnawing hunger, I sat up again, lifting the rucksack on to my knee. I unfastened its strap, wondering what was inside. There, tucked between pockets, were bacon and egg pie, several celery sticks, two red apples, a packet of chocolate wafers and a can of lager. I hadn't eaten bacon and egg pie since schooldays. The can of lager, though reviving, went straight to my head.

I sat there a long time, drawing strength from the silence. The sun was warm, but not too hot. My head cleared as I followed the low flight of cormorants over the sea. Eventually I pulled from my pocket the notebook and ball-point I'd brought with me and wrote a long letter to my Abbess. I knew the community would be waiting for news.

'I've been so grateful for the community's prayers,' I wrote. 'I never imagined my coming to Devon would have turned out as it has, but I still have this persistent sense of having to be here. The hospital confirmed Elizabeth's cancer – they originally gave her a week to live – but there are signs of a remission. I am with her each day, taken to the hospital by kind people in the village. Basil (Elizabeth's husband) is rather infirm – mentally, I suspect, as well as physically – yet also endearing. Nell, a friend of the family, has been wonderfully kind. Her uncle was a monk so she feels she is on familiar ground with me! Kate, the red setter, has been an inseparable companion, though I left her at home today as I was scared she might chase the sheep – they graze up here where I am sitting. Fred would love her. (Does he still lie in his basket at the back of the chapel for Vespers?) I have little time for reading, but always try to manage the Office, and have the Merton book by my bed. There was a good passage last night: "In this tribulation, the love of God is with us, no matter how much we fear." I do feel that. Please give much love to everyone.'

My letter crossed with one from Sister St Richard. I was very glad to hear from her; it was the first letter I'd had. She wrote of everyday events in the convent The runner bean crop had been prolific, everyone spent free time preparing them for freezing. They all missed me, though general discussion of my leave had been discouraged. Fred had got out again, but they'd enticed him back with a particularly succulent bone. She hoped I was eating properly and sent all her love. The community was praying for Elizabeth.

Two days later the nursing officer at the hospital decided Elizabeth might be nursed at home. She was jubilant. Nurses and patients in the adjoining ward congratulated her, genuinely delighted. I pushed her in the chair to the day room. The houseman passed us. 'Ruddy miracle!' he called. We washed her hair. A nurse applied heated rollers and I thought of Monica. Suddenly there was much to be done.

When I told Basil, he brought out a bottle of vintage port.

A meeting was arranged between the district nurse and me. She explained everything clearly, sketching in details of expected nursing, and my role in this. A hospital bed and chair would be delivered to The Hollies. My head was buzzing.

I set about converting the dining room to a bedroom. Elizabeth would be unable to manage stairs. The dining room was stuffed with heavy furniture, cleaned only superficially for several years. The windows were glazed with dust, frames engrained and flaked. I engaged Mrs Tressilian to give me a hand. She worked as a home-help locally, but promised to look in after her other job. Together we moved everything from the room, pushing it into the study on the other side of the hall. I tied a duster to the broomhead and balanced like Eros to bring down cobwebs.

'Might as well be back in the convent!' I laughed as I wobbled to reach a high corner. Mrs Tressilian was intrigued. 'Did you do spring-cleaning, then?' she asked.

I described Mother Joseph, in her eighties, who organised our spring-cleaning year after year till she died. 'She came from Lancashire,' I told her, 'she continued bare-foot from the day she entered, and never let us get away with a thing! In her spare time she made lavender bags which were sold by the gross to Selfridges!'

'Well I never,' said Mrs Tressilian, impressed. She had found the vacuum cleaner, but it was not a recent model. 'Dratted thing don' suck,' she complained.

I discovered some disinfectant, applying it liberally to every surface. Peter called. 'Just like a public lavatory,' he said, making a face. I attacked the windows, the water running down inside my sleeves as I reached for the higher panes. We stopped for mugs of tea, pleased with our progress. Mrs Tressilian said working with me was different.

There was washing to be done. Several of Elizabeth's nightgowns from the hospital awaited attention, also garments from Basil and me. I resolved to tackle the washing machine in the scullery. After a search I found the manual of instruction buried beneath the drying-up cloths in the dresser drawer. The washing powder, under the sink, looked as if it had been there some time but I tipped the recommended amount into the machine. I hoped the lumps would dissolve in the wash. Selecting the programme was more difficult, so I plumped for one that seemed appropriate. The taps and hose connections over the sink were in place. I pressed the relevant buttons and a reassuring sound of circulating water soon followed. I checked my watch. I reckoned it should all be finished by eight-thirty. Basil and I ate dinner.

The mackerel was delicious. I'd cooked it with herbs and lemon, wrapped in a parcel of tinfoil. I'd discovered the recipe in a cookery book behind the egg boxes. It was as I leant forward to gather our plates that I sensed there was something amiss. Dishes in hand, I made at once for the scullery. Rigid with disbelief I came to a halt in the doorway. Below the step the floor was awash with soapy water, suds billowing rhythmically from the base of the washing machine. Spurred into action, I kicked off my sandals and paddled, dumping dishes in the sink as I passed. When reading the manual it hadn't occurred to me to check any emergency stop. I couldn't think what to press. At that moment I heard a click and the whole thing began to shudder. I was horrified. 'Oh, please,' I prayed in desperation, 'please don't blow up . . .'

Basil appeared in the doorway. He looked baffled. 'Oh,' he said. 'Something wrong?'

'I'm just getting the fruit salad,' I lied. It was the first thing that came into my head. Basil's knowledge of washing machines would be even less than my own. He pushed his hand through his hair and turned from the doorway again. I opened the back door and made for the broom. Suddenly the shuddering ceased and the washing machine was silent. No more regurgitations, no more soapy water. I looked at my watch. It was exactly eight-thirty.

Elizabeth really laughed. At the hospital the next morning I sat on the edge of her bed. 'No one told you! We need only half the amount of soap powder down here because the water is soft.'

'We had giant troughs, green soap and a scrubbing board in the convent!' I chided. 'You couldn't see across the wash-house for steam and it took us most of the day!'

Elizabeth apologised. 'I'll soon be home,' she promised.

★

The 2 July was set for her return. The bed, chair and a walking frame had been delivered to The Hollies. Mrs Coombes brought a bunch of roses. Jack, who looked after the garden for Elizabeth, produced peas and beans in a trug. Nell turned up with a baby alarm. 'You'd better have that, dear,' she told me. We draped the wire from its bedside speaker over the banister rail up to my bedroom.

I baked a coffee sponge. Basil wore a clean pullover. Kate, sensing a change, never left my side.

The ambulance arrived at three-thirty. The approach to the house via the garden path was steep. The two men carried the stretcher carefully, negotiating the passageway with skill. Gently they placed Elizabeth on the bed. 'There we go, then!' said the older one. The second retrieved a fallen slipper from the floor. 'All right, love?' he smiled. I offered them tea, but they said they'd best be getting along. We thanked them warmly. Equipment expertly folded, they left with a cheery wave.

'Welcome home!' I greeted Elizabeth, returning to the room. Basil was blowing his nose. Before I could open my mouth to say more, the district nurse arrived. She looked motherly, her face round and smiling. Her bright blue uniform was a little tight fitting. Elizabeth, from her bed, seemed distressed. The nurse turned to her. Instantly professional, she saw to a catheter which was causing discomfort. I went to make tea. Dr Hughes arrived.

Basil and I retired to the sitting room. Elizabeth's homecoming had almost restored his sense of normality. Five minutes later Dr Hughes came through with the nurse. 'I've given her an injection,' he said. 'She'll sleep for a while now. Don't worry if she doesn't eat this evening.'

I made fresh tea. There were flowers everywhere. Everything shone, yet a feeling of anticlimax pervaded the room. We each took a slice of coffee cake. Conversation was stilted, like a scene from Jane Austen. Soon Dr Hughes left, saying he would return tomorrow. Anne, the nurse, stayed a little longer. She, too, would look in the next morning. 'Telephone any time,' she told me. 'During the night, or should you feel anxious – I'll be down straight away.'

I saw her to her car. Walking back to the house I prayed. '*In manus tuam, Domine.*' The Latin came easily, long familiar. Basil had left the sitting room. Dirty tea cups remained where we'd put them down, crumbs from the coffee cake lay where they'd fallen. When I'd stacked everything on to the tray I carried it out to the scullery.

Chapter 6

ELIZABETH CALLED ME ONCE IN THE NIGHT. I heard her through the baby alarm and sped downstairs like lightning.

'I can't get to sleep again,' she said, 'is there any Benger's in the kitchen cupboard?'

I found a half used packet and heated milk. Whilst she sipped it I curled in the large chair near her bed. We hardly spoke; there was no need, the silence was comfortable. It was almost one-thirty, the hour we used to rise for Night Office. After the psalms and readings were finished we'd lie prostrate on the chapel floor, arms out-stretched, praying for those in pain or in any sort of need. I'd often tried to imagine those for whom we interceded. Now I felt on the receiving end, thankful for that unseen support.

I retrieved Elizabeth's empty mug, tucking her up like a child. Back in my room I stood at the open window a while, air cool on my face. In the convent I'd sometimes watched shooting stars tear down the sky after the Night Office. I'd listened to the nightjar's rusty call, but never caught sight of him. Tonight the stars were steady; only a far off sound of the sea broke the still silence. I prayed Elizabeth would sleep.

A day or two later Sue, the second district nurse, suggested we wheel Elizabeth to the sitting room. Wrapped in her Indian blue dressing gown, hair brushed, she sat for an hour whilst Basil and I drank tea with her. She inspected the garden from the open French door, happy to be home. Kate lay sleeping in a patch of sun.

That evening she ate chicken. It was a celebration. Back in bed, she asked me to recite Compline with her. I knelt beside her, my breviary open upon the blanket.

'Save us, Lord, while we are awake,
protect us while we sleep;
that we may keep watch with Christ
and rest with him in peace.'

I reached the final prayer and she joined in. Slowly, with difficulty in remembering, she repeated it with me. 'Stay here and guard us in peace, and let your blessing be always upon us.' We both said Amen, and I laid my hand on her head, making a tiny sign of the cross.

One day soon after this I walked Kate up the valley. Foxgloves were over now, ferns and tall grasses replacing them. I was glad of the overgrown valley which made a cool shade. I threw a stick for Kate which she tore after to retrieve. She dived into a stagnant pool we passed, her drenched red coat bedecked like Ophelia as she swam in blissful satisfaction. I wished we need not turn back. We called into the village stores for stamps. I did not know the name of the postmistress; she was referred to by everyone as 'The Post Office'. The sun was still hot as we climbed up from the lane. Outside the back door the clothes-line held two night-gowns and a tea towel, all bone dry. I heard Elizabeth's voice from her room as I unpegged them.

'I think Basil's fallen,' she called. 'I can't get out of bed alone – I think he's in the front hall.'

I flew into the house. Basil lay sprawled on the tiled floor. I squatted beside him, fearing he'd broken a bone and afraid to move him. I rang Dr Hughes. It was his day off, but the secretary promised to tell the doctor on duty. When I returned to the hall, Basil was struggling to get up. I took what weight I could and heaved him on to a hall chair. His face was grey and I remembered Dr Hughes' anxiety. By now he could speak. He cursed himself for his stupidity.

'Don't move off that chair!' I admonished, praying the doctor would hurry.

He looked at me as Kate had done. It hurt to see it. Then he asked for a cup of tea. I appealed to Elizabeth. Should he drink tea? She thought he might so I made a pot and took a cup to Basil, placing it on the third stair nearest the chair on which he sat. He took a sip and seemed to recover a little. I stood beside him, on hand to take the cup. As I did so he looked up and said with urgency, 'I want to pee.' Help, I thought. I was unused to this. I hurried through to Elizabeth. 'There's a bottle on the top shelf of the hot cupboard,' she told me. As I raced from her room I heard her call after me, 'You'll need to stand on the bathroom stool.' I clambered past the cup and saucer and found the bottle in the hot cupboard. Running downstairs again, I thrust it at Basil, hoping he could manage the rest. At that moment there was a tap on the open front door. The duty doctor appeared round it, carrying his doctor's bag. To me, it seemed as if he were the archangel Gabriel himself. He strode across to Basil. The half drunk tea rested on the third stair side by side with the used bottle. It was too late to move them. Basil, the doctor said, had suffered a temporary slight stroke. It would probably clear after a while but he suggested we make up a bed for him on the ground floor. He gave Basil a pill to take and helped him to his chair in the sitting room. He was very kind. After a while, and after a word to Elizabeth, he picked up his bag. 'I'll tell Dr Hughes,' he assured us. Then, turning to me, he said, 'I'm sure the district nurse will give you a hand with Basil.'

It was the young nurse Sue who came. She shared my shock, but was also practical. As soon as she'd greeted Elizabeth and seen to her medicine, she helped me down with Basil's bed. As we angled it round the bend of the stairs I was thankful for all the furniture we'd moved in the convent – there were never any men to give help. We decided to put the bed in the study, shifting up to one end chairs, tables, china, books and assorted pictures stuffed there since the previous conversion of the dining-room. A large ornately covered Victorian screen made a handy partition.

Sue undressed Basil. She helped him to his new bedroom. He lay propped up in bed wearing his blue pyjamas, apologising for the inconvenience he'd caused. After Sue had left, I stayed with him until he relaxed and his eyes closed. When he slept I tiptoed away to prepare supper for Elizabeth. She was clearly worried about Basil, despite my effort to sound reassuring.

That night she was very restless. Nothing seemed to alleviate this and I knew she was also in pain. Eventually, at ten to three in the morning, I rang Dr Hughes. He was on duty again and answered at once. 'Right,' he said, 'I'll be with you in fifteen minutes.'

As soon as he arrived he went swiftly to Elizabeth. He was very gentle. Then he turned to me. 'I think we are going to teach you to give an injection!' he said. My heart sank. I felt totally ill-equipped for such a role. Dr Hughes was emphatic. 'You can do it!' he smiled.

He opened his case and extracted a syringe. I looked at Elizabeth. I knew she would sense my misgiving. With a weak smile she whispered, 'Go on – I'll tell you if you hurt!'

Doctor Hughes made me have a practice shot. I injected an orange from the bowl on the table. He demonstrated how air was expelled first, and how to insert the needle swiftly and firmly. He then took

Elizabeth's arm and handed me the prepared syringe. He ordered me to give the injection. I glanced at Elizabeth then plunged the needle into her arm. I was numb with fright. Elizabeth's eyes were closed.

'Brave girl,' she murmured.

Dr Hughes, more prosaic, said, 'There you are! That wasn't too difficult, was it?'

Had he but known.

After that I gradually became accustomed to giving injections when these became necessary. Doctor Hughes left me a supply of stronger drugs for which I had to sign a book each time they were administered. Without the district nurses I should never have managed. Sue said The Hollies was becoming a hospice.

'That's not what I envisaged!' I laughed. Visitors called. I made cakes for their tea and arranged all the flowers they brought. Michael, the vicar, came regularly. So did Nell.

The community became used to my telephone calls for prayer. They were genuinely concerned, my Abbess taken by surprise at this unexpected outcome. I remembered a phrase learned in noviciate days: 'Grace builds on nature'. It had taken me years to appreciate what this might mean, but I began at last to sense an indication of it in these unforeseen events. With something of the chameleon in my nature, I supposed I was being given the strength and requisite grace to adapt to them. I was certainly aware of support.

Some evenings Peter brought Gully, a Tibetan sheepdog, to see Elizabeth. She loved Peter. Gully too, brought her pleasure. Basil would come through from the sitting room, staying with us until dusk became darkness and we could no longer see. Peace enfolded us. In sadder moments I wondered how long it could be sustained. It was only a few more days before I found out.

Chapter 7

DOCTOR HUGHES HAD WARNED that Elizabeth's remission might not last. On the morning of 25 July she had been unable to keep down food. She was in pain and looked ill. 'I'm not going to make it, you know,' she said without emotion.

I sat on her bed, wishing I might pretend.

'I think you may possibly be right,' I said as gently as I could, 'but don't think of it as the end – you know what we said about the continuity of the spirit. If this bit has to go it's only because the moment has come to shed the chrysalis of the body. You – the you created by God for all eternity – can never die from physical illness.'

She looked at me without speaking, holding my hand. I was less brave than I sounded. I'd come to cherish the hope of her recovery, of our triumph over her cancer. I remembered the houseman's words at the hospital: 'I think it will be only a matter of days.' I'd wanted to prove him wrong. It had taken weeks rather than days but that was of little comfort. After a while, still looking at me, Elizabeth said, 'I want to be received into the Catholic Church.'

I was categoric. 'Not because of me, please . . .'

'No!' she managed a smile. 'Not because of you – Aunt B became a Catholic before she died. I feel the same. I know I must –'

I knew Aunt B had been Peter's grandmother. He'd told me she was Elizabeth's favourite aunt.

'What do you want me to do, then?' I asked.

'Get Father Nolan!' she begged.

She lay back exhausted. I released my hand, easing her down to a more comfortable position. Just as I turned from the bed she called me again. 'Say the Jesus prayer you taught me – I want to say it now, with you.'

I knelt beside the bed. She tried to join in as I repeated the words. Someone had sent them to me years before and I kept the parchment card in my breviary:

48

Jesus be thou in me that other souls may find,
not my estrangéd mind repelling ruthlessly,
but find thee, Jesus, thee, looking from my eyes,
tender, beneficent, wise.

I recited the words slowly, Elizabeth struggling to keep up. She looked happy. 'That's it,' she whispered. 'That's how it must always be . . .' I crept from the room, my throat constricted.

I spoke to Basil before ringing Father Nolan. 'Elizabeth has asked to become a Catholic,' I told him. 'Do you mind if I ask a priest to come?'

Basil was amazed that I should consult him. He had always acquiesced in matters concerning Elizabeth's Christian belief. For once he was quite coherent. 'Of course not!' he said.

I telephoned Michael first. I knew, as her vicar, he should be consulted over such a proposed move. He came at once on his motorcycle. Dumping his helmet and anorak in the hall he made straight for Elizabeth's room. I left them together and went to make coffee. Before the kettle had boiled he came through to me in the kitchen. He perched on the edge of the table. 'I'm in no doubt that this is what she wants,' he said. 'I only wish these "divisions" were unnecessary. The important thing now, though, is for whatever brings peace to her soul. On that score I am happy for you to call a Roman priest.'

Nick and Julie were with their families. I didn't think they would object. Basil was sure they would not. I telephoned Father Nolan. He remembered me and promised to come about four o'clock the next afternoon. I gave him directions to The Hollies.

The following morning Anne, the district nurse, helped Elizabeth into a clean nightgown. I tidied the room and asked Jack for fresh flowers. Basil sat glued to the cricket on his television, immured in the sitting room.

When I heard his car I walked across the garden to meet Father Nolan. He carried a stole over his arm and a small case in the other hand.

'Thank you so much for coming,' I greeted him. 'This time I believe Elizabeth is quite certain. She begged me to get you in person!'

I led him to Elizabeth, whose frailty was marked. Unpacking his case, he placed what he needed on the table I'd prepared by her bed.

He asked only the minimum of questions. When he'd administered the rites of the sick and dying he signed to me to receive half the communion host. I knelt where she could see me in case she needed that assurance.

'This is the Lamb of God,' said Father Nolan, lifting the wafer before us. 'Who takes away the sins of the world . . .'

'*Domine, non sum dignus* . . .' I added to myself.

The priest broke the wafer. He placed half on Elizabeth's tongue. 'The Body of Christ,' he repeated.

'Amen,' I whispered. I said it for both of us.

Father Nolan removed his stole. He re-packed in his case the oils and silver pyx that had contained the communion host. He smiled at Elizabeth. 'God bless you,' he said with compassion. 'You have all you need for the journey now. Be at peace.'

I took him to meet Basil, who was delighted. 'Glad you came,' Basil said. 'Are you a cricketer?'

I offered him tea but he declined. 'I have to be back by five-thirty,' he smiled. 'Let me know if you need anything.'

I escorted him to his car, handing him an envelope in which I'd enclosed an offering. 'Now you don't need to give me that,' he protested, suddenly Irish.

'Keep us in your prayers,' I said. 'I can seldom get to Mass.'

'Aren't you living the Mass?' he chided me gently. With a wave from the open window he started the car. ''Bye now – take care!'

I returned to Elizabeth. She was, I thought, asleep, her face radiant. She opened her eyes as I entered the room. They were shining. 'There's only Love,' she said softly. She lifted her thin hand up to my face. 'It's true, you know – there's only Love, only Love –'

Three days later it became clear she was dying. For the past ten days I'd slept on a sofa in her room, on hand should she require help or a further injection. Some nights there was little chance of sleep. Once, she had woken to say quite distinctly, 'I'm so happy, so much at peace.' Then she'd added, 'There are so many people – I can see so many loving faces . . .'

I'd thought of the Letter to the Hebrews, 'We are surrounded by so great a cloud of witnesses . . .' For Elizabeth, did it matter that this might be also an effect of diamorphine? I remembered old Sister Rose in the community. She hadn't been on morphine. Just before she died she'd raised herself from the pillow with an unforgettable smile. 'Wait for me!' she'd cried. 'Wait for me – I'm coming, I'm coming –'

Two or three times one of the nurses had stayed a night to give me rest, but Sue warned me that Elizabeth would be unlikely to survive today. The date was 2 August, the anniversary of the founding of our Order in Assisi. What Saint Francis had begun in the tiny chapel of the Portincola had been honoured with devotion since the thirteenth century. This day, for me, was of special significance. For Elizabeth, too, with her affection for Saint Francis, I saw a fitting pattern. Her deterioration suddenly became rapid. We telephoned for Nick and Julie. Together Sue and I made sure we had done everything we could. Dr Hughes, who had come earlier, was unable to do more now. I told Sue I would sit beside Elizabeth whilst she slipped home for an hour. She had a young family. Basil preferred to stay in the sitting room. I read aloud quietly the prayers for the dying.

'I entrust you to God who created you. May you return to the one who formed you from the dust of the earth. May Mary, the angels, and all the saints, come to meet you as you go forth from this life.' I knew she would have wanted that. I think I felt like a midwife. I longed for her to have a safe delivery. 'Relax,' I whispered to her unconscious form. 'Allow death to come – your spirit will soon be free –'

When it came, she gave only a tiny sigh, light as a snowflake. She looked totally at peace. It was four-fifteen in the afternoon.

Basil was inconsolable.

Sue had returned as soon as I'd rung. A cousin of Elizabeth, staying in the village, sat with us into the evening. Dr Hughes came and left again, undertakers would be calling in the morning. Telephone calls had to be made, relatives told. Nick and Julie, so recently here but reluctantly just returned home, now postponed their arrival until the funeral.

I sat on the hearthrug at Basil's feet trying to comfort as best I could. His grief helped assuage mine. We toyed with a little food, finding it tasteless.

At length, visitors gone, I edged Basil towards his bed. Though now able to walk, he still slept downstairs, recently beset by incontinence. 'My bloody bowels ...' he would groan as another disaster occurred. It caused him much distress. I helped him undress and tucked him under the duvet. I gave him his night pill and placed a glass of water on the table beside him. The tumbler of whisky remained almost untouched in the sitting room. 'Goodnight, darling,' I said. 'I'm here. I won't leave you.'

Moments later, as I stood at the scullery door waiting for Kate, I wondered what the community would think about that.

There was much to be done. Nell took me to both registrar and undertaker. She rode through every formality. 'No good saying it wasn't for the best, dear,' she said frankly. 'What sort of life would she have had? Waste of yours too. Basil will be happy with you there – he'll be all right.'

Her last remark only confirmed what I'd begun to suspect. With Elizabeth's death I had lost my original reason for remaining at The Hollies, yet I knew I could not desert Basil.

'I'll be up to see him at six,' Nell promised as she dropped me at the bottom of the lane.

The telephone rang incessantly. Relatives made arrangements for attending the funeral, villagers called with messages of sympathy. Avril came down from her caravan park, customary brightness replaced by genuine grief. She brought cartons of hazelnut ice cream. Sometimes the fact of Elizabeth's dying came home to me unbearably. Self-pity became leaden. Why had this happened? Why had I felt compelled to ask for my leave of absence to come to – this? Never, not even for a day, had I known her active presence, robust and healthy, at The Hollies. Everywhere I turned there were only the marks of her having lived there, never herself. The kitchen held utensils I'd never seen her handle; her knitting bag, work half finished, still lay where she'd left it on a stool in the sitting room. A bedside drawer revealed pencil stubs, notebooks, safety pins, lipstick and a partly filled diary for 1979. 'Why?' I raged, 'why this implacable denial of our plans?'

I slipped from the house to give Kate a walk. I knew where I wanted to take her. We climbed the path above the inlet where I'd eaten Nell's picnic. I sank on to the cropped turf while Kate raced ahead. There were no sheep. The sky was cloudless, sunlight reflecting from the sea. Nothing broke the silence. Kate investigated scents that intrigued her, then ran back, flopping beside me. Quite suddenly I was so aware of Elizabeth's presence that I actually looked round. The sensation was immediate and indisputable. I felt a joy beyond description, for she was far closer than I'd ever known her. It seemed as if her smile, her voice, her whole being were alive within my own. Any doubt of her continuing spiritual reality instantly dissolved. I felt radiant. 'All we have lost is the fear of losing,' I remembered from somewhere. I reached out my hand to Kate as we remained there, immobile and convinced, until the sun lost its warmth. It was a long time before we at last retraced our steps to the village.

The funeral was to be taken by Elizabeth's Anglican cousin, Bishop Paul. The instruction for this had been left in her will. I spoke to Father Nolan who suggested we had a private Requiem later. Paul, when I told him, agreed with this.

Wanting to be kind, Nell asked me to help with flowers for the little church. Together we filled glass carboys with everything from the herbaceous border that Jack allowed. 'You take all them dahlias,' he told me with untypical magnanimity. I filled the house with flowers too. Everyone would be returning there after the funeral.

It was imperative Basil take a bath. He had developed a disinclination to make any contact with water. I knew he must change into a suit for the occasion. I summoned Peter. 'Could you possibly organise a bath for Basil?' I asked. I sounded like my Abbess, no question of refusal. Peter grinned. I knew he wouldn't mind. I took Basil's dark suit from the cupboard and placed clean towels in the bathroom. Sue, still calling to see him regularly, provided a pair of waterproof underpants. I heard the bathwater running. Peter, sleeves rolled up, was in attendance. Some while later I heard him call from the landing.

'Success with the bath!' he declared, 'but we do have a spot of bother on the next lap – he's asking for you!'

I ran up to the bathroom. Through the steam emerging from the open door I saw Basil seated on the bathroom stool, swathed in towels. In his hands he held the waterproof underpants. He was inspecting them with disdain. 'And what,' he said, 'am I to do with these?'

I hadn't looked at them myself. I hadn't thought about it. I had no idea they were made without an opening. Basil looked flummoxed. My abbatial authority evaporated in the steam. 'All right!' I apologised, 'I'll find one of your usual pairs!'

Peter was laughing.

The bell, light as a school bell, rang from the small belfry of the village church. Cars carried us the short distance to the porch. Basil insisted I enter on his arm. Nick and Julie were already seated, cousins and friends packed the remaining pews. Basil and I made our way to the front where seats were reserved for us. A posy of wild flowers I'd made lay beside wreaths on the coffin. The service took its course. Paul spoke affectionately of his cousin Elizabeth. He remembered long summer holidays spent with her family, early memories of Elizabeth before her first marriage. He recalled tragic wartime deaths and brave feats of young fighter pilot cousins. I dared not look at Basil.

When it was done I left him with Nell. She and Basil were returning with visitors for tea at The Hollies. We'd spent the morning making sandwiches and cakes, rearranging the sitting room to accommodate those coming back to the house. Only Nick, Julie and I, with a close family friend, went to Barnstaple for the cremation that followed the service. I knew Father Nolan would not question this. For some time now cremation had been allowed for Catholics. Michael was at the impersonal chapel to meet us. The committal was formal and very brief.

Nick and Julie stayed on a few days. They invited me to remain at the house as long as I wished. I accepted this gratefully. Quite apart from the question of Basil, I thought it probably sensible. I needed time to think out my future. Three days after the funeral Julie and I collected Elizabeth's ashes from the crematorium. Peter was rowing out beyond the headland, where Elizabeth had requested her ashes be cast into the sea. Julie asked me to go with them. It was the least I could do. The sea was calm, greenly translucent. While Peter rested on his oars, I emptied the urn, devoid of feeling. Words, inappropriate now, were postponed till later.

Extinguished?
You?
That bright flame quenched?
Fool!
Pain's blade severs –
but not the spirit!
Closed eyes smile, sparked by eternity,
(indelible joy)

and the spirit soars, free as a bird,
and timeless are the moments
etched on the soul's spun memory –
thistledown light, coloured strand of the wave –
Sunlight, and diamond tears
and the path stands empty?
　　Ah, that . . .
Love is the calligraphy of everlasting life.

Basil and I settled into a routine. He disliked me leaving him alone for more than a few minutes. If in another room he'd call frequently, asking if I were there. Paul wrote suggesting a nursing home. He reminded me that Basil might live like this for years. I too had thought of this. I'd written, describing the funeral, to Sister St Richard.

'Funny,' I wrote, 'that in my youth I expect I'd have given my socks to say "Darling I'll never leave you" to a chosen suitor! Now, here I am with Basil, safeguarded – as if that were necessary – by a vow of chastity! How well I remember your admonition, "Man

Basil

proposes, God disposes" – there's quite a bit of "disposing" taking place now – it makes for an eventful life! Do pray that I'm sufficiently adaptable . . .'

Doctor Hughes called, wondering if I'd consider running The Hollies as a hospice. I remembered Nurse Sue. Basil actually recalled our original idea for the house to be used for a place of spiritual retreat and renewal. The Hollies was his now, left him by Elizabeth for his lifetime. 'You do what you like,' he told me again and again. 'I won't stand in your way! It's what Elizabeth wanted.' I ached for Basil, so anxious to help. I believe at last he was almost happy. He preferred to eat lunch with me now, rarely going further than the garden to talk with Jack. Nell's visits cheered him each evening, a ritual for both of them.

'That swine from the hotel blocked my drive with his minibus,' Nell announced with her second whisky. We found ourselves nearly laughing again. Nell was sure I should take a holiday. Just as she'd badgered me about leaving Elizabeth in the hospital, she confronted me now about a few days away from Basil. 'You must, dear,' she said. 'You know perfectly well Peter and I can look after him while you have a break. Cherry can come over too.' Cherry ran the inn, I knew Basil liked her. Once again I eventually gave in to her bludgeoning.

I wrote to an old friend in Penzance, arranging a time she could manage. It was to be a weekend. Peter offered to take me by car to catch the train from Exeter. All that week Basil was restless, glad I should go yet dreading my not being there. He insisted on paying for my ticket, again and again asking, 'Are you certain you're all right for money?' Meticulously faithful to Elizabeth's request, he had always maintained the housekeeping purse. I could have spent far more than I needed.

Friday came and I checked the supply of whisky and refilled the jug with fresh water. I made up bottles of tonic with the help of a noisy machine for Nell's lunch-time gin. I put out clean clothing and wrote endless notes beside Basil's essential pills. I tried to explain to Kate that I'd be back soon.

Peter came down from the lane. His eyes were blue, almost as blue as Elizabeth's.

He greeted Basil and picked up the bag I'd borrowed from Nell. 'Won't be long, Basil!' he said as he stood in the hall. I'd given Basil a kiss, but blew him another.

'Back Sunday night!' I called. 'Cherry and Nell will be there!'

He watched me go. Kate stood beside him, expressive eyes resigned to my departure. I felt I was deserting them both. I prayed I'd left everything out for Cherry.

Chapter 8

IT WAS A LOVELY RUN TO EXETER. Peter pointed out a heron which rose from a water meadow, hunched and unhurried on huge ragged wings. I remembered the heron that ate up the goldfish in the convent pond. I'd come down at five on my way to the chapel one morning and saw him perched on the edge. When he heard me he'd taken off, most of the fish with him. 'Probably the same heron, come to provoke you!' smiled Peter.

He carried my bag to the platform when we reached Exeter, waving me off on the train. The last time I'd travelled to Cornwall the train had been powered by steam. This diesel took only five hours from London to Penzance. I sat in one of the four facing seats divided by a table. Where the track ran along by the sea I was reminded of the Mediterranean. It was years since I'd been on a holiday. I was thankful to be alone although I felt vulnerable, unused to travel by myself. There was time to observe, to enjoy the distantly remembered countryside as it sped past the window. I was tempted to search for the buffet car, assailed by a thirst for coffee that I'd seen someone carry to their seat, but courage failed me. Only necessity spurred me to make my way to the WC.

Madeleine met me at Penzance. She lived in a tiny whitewashed cottage not far from the quay. I'd last seen her when she stayed at the convent; she knew nothing of The Hollies. She was amazed at what I told her.

'Well at least you showed a modicum of sanity getting out,' she observed. 'How you could stand all those women for so long defies reason.'

'I haven't "got out"!' I protested. 'I simply tried to follow what seemed like a distinct "second call".' I sounded like a tract, but was too tired to care.

Madeleine raised her eyes in disbelief, reaching for her Noilly Prat.

'What *you* need is some intellectual stimulus!' she told me bluntly.

We walked to Newlyn discussing art, sat listening to recordings of Mahler. She read me forgotten translations of Maritain, quoted lines from Claudel. In the evenings we sat in her tiny yard with a bottle of wine. We ate dressed avocados and delicious pasta, with salad served from an Italian pottery bowl. I hadn't lived like this since leaving home, years ago. The two days sped.

'I must say you've certainly landed yourself in a bizarre situation now, but I don't doubt you'll survive,' Madeleine told me as we walked to the station on the Sunday afternoon. 'Read Dostoevsky again – *Brothers Karamazov* – can't remember which chapter. Starts off: "Love will teach us all things . . ." marvellous passage.'

I left Penzance with a certain reluctance. It had revived me; I felt better. Madeleine handed me a copy of *The Tablet*. 'Good article on Newman,' she said, still pursuing my intellectual stimulus. As the train slid into the platform she gave me a kiss on both cheeks. 'Come back when you can't stand any more!' she commanded.

Peter was waiting at Exeter. I was glad to think of the fifty miles run; it would give me space to adjust. Peter stooped for my bag, greeting me warmly. Together we threaded our way through waiting passengers. As we emerged from the station he turned to look down at me, speaking hesitantly.

'I have something to tell you . . .' He started again, his face grave. 'There's been a bit of a shock – I have to tell you – I'm very sorry to say . . .' at last he came out with what he wanted to say, 'that Basil died yesterday morning.'

I was speechless.

'We didn't ring you,' Peter continued. 'We knew it could make no difference. We thought it more sense that you take what was left of your weekend.' Peter recounted the past twenty-four hours as we drove. Cherry had brought Basil's coffee at about eleven. Just when he'd finished it, his colour noticeably changed. Worried, she'd rung Dr Hughes, but Basil had died in his chair before the doctor arrived. It was very swift, Peter said. Nick and Julie had been summoned again. Julie, now arrived, was seeing to everything. My head reeled. It was only two weeks since Elizabeth's death. Dear Basil. At least he hadn't had long to live without her. I wondered whether he would have died had I not been away, but speculation of that kind was futile. Words from the thirteenth century anchoress, Julian of Norwich, flashed into my head. 'Nothing is by hap nor by adventure.' I'd have liked to believe that.

The Hollies seemed awash with people, the sitting room cloudy with cigarette smoke. Julie, Cherry and Michael with two of their friends, all talking over their drinks. When Peter and I walked in the conversation stopped. I felt an intruder. Then everyone smiled, suddenly animated again as if they were clockwork, retelling the dramatic events of Sunday. Peter poured me sherry, helping himself to whisky. I tried hard to respond but my heart rebelled, overcome by a longing for silence. As soon as I decently could I excused myself, saying goodnight before going upstairs to my room.

Shattered, I knelt with my head on the seat of the ancient armchair. I wept, instinctively fearful for whatever might lie ahead. The arms of the chair were threadbare, stuffing protruding from holes in the worst worn parts. I noticed this as I stopped to blow my nose. With concentration I poked back some of the broken threads. Tonight there were no interior nudgings, nothing but darkness as far as I could see. I wished my Abbess or Sister St Richard were there to give me counsel, but it was too late to telephone now. I felt drenched with tiredness. Over the next few days all the formalities of a fortnight ago were repeated. This time it was Julie, not Nell, who went to inform the registrar. Arrangements with the undertaker were more complex. Basil, in keeping with his naval tradition, had desired his burial at sea. 'No hope of any help from the navy now,' we were told. 'You'll have to arrange your own vessel.' Nick was advised to get in touch with the man who ran the local pleasure boat. The man said he'd like to oblige, but everything depended on his set times for trippers. After lengthy negotiations they reached an agreement, settling for 21 August. 'Eight-thirty sharp that morning,' stressed the man.

The day dawned overcast, threatening rain. Only a few of us stood on the quayside. Most of the family felt unable to return so soon for another funeral. Basil had no one of his own. Nell would miss him, so would Peter and Cherry, but he'd lived at The Hollies too short a time for villagers really to know him. The wind blowing off the sea was chill as we huddled beside ropes and nets festooning the harbour wall. Nick smoked a cigarette. Julie, in jeans and a sweater, talked quietly with Peter and Cherry. Nell, dressed for the weather, determined to pay her last respects to Basil, held my arm.

The skipper arrived, jaunty fisherman's cap a sign of his authority. He signalled for us to embark. Obediently, one by one, we walked the bouncing gangplank. Four men from the undertaker, solemn in overcoats and gloves, bore Basil's coffin to its place astern in the cockpit. They draped it with a Union Jack and took their seats behind it, squashed tightly together upon a transverse bench.

Michael was to officiate. As we took our seats beneath the canvas awning I felt Nell prod my ribs. I looked round. I saw Michael, just arrived, bounding on to the boat. He was attired, as he later explained, in the uniform of a Sea Cadet padre, a tribute to Basil's naval connections. He wore his white-topped cap at a fetching Admiral Beatty angle. Nell's mirth was contagious; I dared not catch Peter's eye.

We drew away from the quay. Beyond the harbour bar waves were crested with foam and spray. It wouldn't have surprised me to hear the skipper point out tourist attractions along the coast. The boat pitched and tossed, dipped and rose again as we headed out to sea. Julie, seated opposite, looked green. The four undertaker's men sat unrealistically passive. We continued on our course for almost half an hour. 'Basil will be enjoying this!' Nell whispered hoarsely into my ear. At length the engine quietened and we moved only as the swell dictated. I was thankful I'd always been a good sailor.

Michael removed his cap. He stood with one hand holding the central pole which supported the awning. With his free hand he produced a stole from his pocket, momentarily loosening his grip in order to adjust the stole over his jacket. He began the funeral service.

Responses to the prayers were almost lost in the strong breeze. We closed our eyes. Michael reached the final rites for the disposal of the coffin. We did our best to turn towards the undertaker's men now preparing, with caution, to release it. Positioning eventually achieved, they slid the coffin into the waves, retrieving the Union Jack in the nick of time. Wreaths from us all were cast on the water at once. We stood in homage but with difficulty. The engine started again. The skipper turned his boat for home. Nobody spoke; the need for dry land was too pressing. Rain lashed the awning; our faces were stung by the wind. Michael, now greener than Julie, sat with his face to the rail. Peter, at home on the sea, remained impervious. I hated leaving Basil to these merciless depths, but his wishes had been carried out. He'd been committed, as he wanted, to his final resting place. I prayed Elizabeth would be waiting. When we reached the shore Nick offered us brandy. Everyone needed it. I raised the tot of reviving liquid to my lips in silent tribute. Basil and I had shared many vicissitudes. This one I was going to find particularly difficult to forget.

Chapter 9

AFTER BASIL'S FUNERAL, NICK AND JULIE decided to sell The Hollies. It was now theirs.

Elizabeth had updated her existing will when she'd learned of her illness. She had called her solicitor, begging me to stay in the room whilst he sat by her bedside, notebook in hand. Turning to me, she'd asked, 'Shall I leave The Hollies to you? You could develop the place along our lines if I don't recover.'

'Of course you mustn't do that!' I'd told her emphatically.

My leave of absence only released me from religious vows until I'd determined my future. Quite apart from this, I was sure the house should belong to the children. Elizabeth, I knew, had thought only of fulfilling our dream. She'd compromised in the end by leaving the house in the care of Basil until his own death.

'Stay till The Hollies is sold, if you like,' Nick invited.

I was also sure this wasn't feasible. They were grateful I'd been there whilst Elizabeth was ill, but any usefulness I might have had was peripheral with Basil dead. They would never have voiced this. It needed no saying. I was uncertain what to do. Doubt seeped into every crevice. Like a house of cards, The Hollies and all I'd believed predestined had collapsed about me. I wondered if I had wholly misinterpreted the sense of vocation I'd felt that July morning in the convent garden. Suddenly I found myself racked with a raw futility I'd never known before.

I did not ask to return to the community, nor did my Abbess suggest it. I spurred myself with a remembered verse from Deuteronomy. 'You saw how he brought you safely to this place, just as a father would carry his son . . .' The application of the Israelites' exodus from Egypt to my own plight could be stretching a point, but the overall thought gave me comfort. I needed faith. Nick offered me Elizabeth's Volkswagen Beetle. 'She'd like you to have it,' he smiled. I did not turn this down. I had little hope of affording to run it, nor had I yet driven again, but I asked if I might sell the car. Nick agreed. He knew someone who wanted it. Suddenly I would have £600 to see me on my way.

At times I felt almost an onlooker. Only Kate remained a link with
The Hollies as I knew it. I took her for walks, even once with Avril.
Avril picked us up in her dilapidated Ford, taking us to Woolacombe,
where we parked above sand dunes before making our way to the
shore. Beyond the dunes, I watched Kate tear along the wet sand. I
could scarcely bring myself to catch her eye these days. Nick was
taking her home with him; I knew she would be well looked after,
but that didn't ease my heart.

I tried to think where I might actually take myself.

'Why don't you try for a mobile home?' Avril suggested as she
limped beside me through the undergrowth. 'They're wonderfully
cosy! What fun we'd be able to have!'

Ambrose had kept in touch. One evening he telephoned from
Sussex. 'Come back to us,' he offered, before Monica took over the
receiver. 'Your room is all ready for you, darling!' she echoed down
the line. The smile behind her spectacles was easy to picture. I should
have guessed they would be likely to come up with something.
They'd never hesitated, whoever might be in need. I was near to
tears.

'Oh, that would be such a relief,' I found myself confessing.

'Then we'll expect you in a week from now!' they confirmed. Julie
lent me Basil's tin trunk for my belongings. It held his uniform, a
Gieves & Hawkes label still in place on the lid. We laid everything,
including his sword, on the longest shelf of the Victorian mahogany
cupboard. The typewriter, my engraving tools, and anything I could
not pack, I labelled and stacked for removal later. Peter kindly said
he would come up to Sussex in the next few months. We sent the
tin trunk by carrier.

Nick and Julie sorted furniture and household goods. Items were
earmarked for eventual removal later. No one stopped to cook; meals
were brought in from the nearest supermarket, consumed on a corner
of the kitchen table or a rug spread out on the lawn. Heat was
suddenly oppressive.

Nell walked up to the house. 'You're getting out of this,' she
announced. 'I'm giving you a rest before you leave. Come down
tomorrow!' I did not argue. Nick and Julie were too occupied to
comment. The thought of leaving Kate haunted me. She and I had
drawn comfort from one another since the onset of Elizabeth's illness.
Together we'd witnessed her death and Basil's, the disintegration of

all we had taken for granted. Now we were to lose each other. I tried to explain, counting on her canine intuition.

'You'll be all right with Nick,' I told her. 'He'll take you for wonderful walks.'

I took her a final walk with me. We climbed the wooded valley, past the stagnant pool she could never resist. She ran back to where I sat on a fallen tree, shaking the stinking water from her chestnut coat. I produced a biscuit from my pocket. She held up a paw and tears suddenly pricked my eyes. 'Oh Kate, you've been such a friend – I'm sorry.' I hugged her damp smelly head. Then I pulled myself to my feet and started off down the path. Unable to look at her I picked up a stick and threw it for her. 'Race you back then,' I croaked, as she overtook me, lolloping over the stony track.

During the evening I selected the suitcase with hinges minus a latch, packed it with what hadn't gone into the trunk and secured it with rope. Nick carried it for me when I left just before lunch the following day. We crossed the plank bridge over the little stream and down the lane to Nell's house. She came from her porch to meet us. The little poodle barked. 'There you are, dear,' she said. 'Come in. Lunch is ready.'

Smiling, Nick dumped the case. He bent to give me a kiss. 'See you soon," he said, before saying goodbye to Nell. I watched as he strode down the path. Nell refused to let me lift a finger. Overfed, I pleaded for less food, but she was adamant. She cooked steak and mounds of vegetables from her garden. She plied me with puddings and cake, brought Horlicks for me at bedtime. I slept and slept. One day Peter asked me to accompany him fishing. He came for me after lunch. In the boat, I sat with my back to the prow, facing him at the tiller. We spoke little because of the noise from the outboard engine.

'Have a shot at trolling!' Peter shouted, handing across to me the trolling line beside him. I let it run behind us, as he instructed. Soon I felt an unmistakable tug. I signalled urgently to Peter.

'Wind in the line!' he called. Slowly, with unbelievable satisfaction, I saw the silver-blue mackerel break surface. It splashed and fought and still I felt only exhilaration. Peter leaned over to retrieve the fish. He dealt with it swiftly, using only one hand, tossing it into the well of the boat. I was astonished at my sense of achievement.

'Well done!' Peter congratulated me, 'try again!' I caught four more mackerel.

When we reached the jetty, I thanked him. 'That was lovely.'

'We'll do it again,' he smiled. 'You'll just have to come back one day.'

Nell had promised to take me to a hairdresser. My hair, in urgent need of attention before the effect of sea spray, was by now beyond recall. I asked Nell where I should go. We drove to Barnstaple.

'This one should do,' said Nell, as we managed to park by an obvious hairdressing establishment. 'I'll pick you up in an hour.'

It had cost three and six when I'd visited a hairdresser last. There were no remembered cubicles here. The girl led me to a seat and washed my hair backwards over the basin. When she'd wrapped my head in towels, she showed me to another chair with fellow customers on either side. She took scissors and comb and began to attack my damp white locks. 'Like it layered?' she enquired.

I'd no idea what she meant. 'Oh, yes please!' I said hopefully.

She pruned and trimmed. I hoped she thought I'd returned from Outer Mongolia.

From time to time she surveyed her handiwork in the glass before me. She was pretty, and looked at herself as well as me. 'Don't like criticising work of other hair stylists,' she observed confidentially, 'but whoever did yours last time never did you a service.'

Nell thought the result a vast improvement.

Peter had a brother-in-law staying for the weekend. He planned to return to London on the Monday evening. Peter was going with him. They offered me a lift. 'It will set you on your way to Sussex,' suggested Peter. 'You can stay the night with us and catch a train from Victoria next morning.'

It seemed sensible. Nell encouraged me to accept. 'Much more comfortable, dear,' she said.

I re-packed my case. I wrapped cottonwool round the cowry shells we'd found in the sand near Woolacombe. 'Keep those!' Nell commanded. 'They'll bring you back one day!' I engraved a small glass for Nell in gratitude for my stay, presenting it to her just before the car was due. She looked pleased. I'd inscribed her name on the glass, surrounding it with a design of the fuchsia she loved. 'Darling, that's lovely!' she said. She wanted to make up a parcel of stores to take with me, but I remembered the bin liners I'd stuffed into Julie's car. 'I feel totally restored – and not a little overweight!'

'Come back soon!' she called as we moved off. 'You know I'm always here.'

We moved fast up the steep, twisting lane. Late evening light cast a stillness over the bay. If we spoke, it was politely. I wondered what lay ahead for me. 'If I die,' Elizabeth had said, 'never worry. I'll be working with you.' At the time, I'd retorted, 'All right for you,' yet only three weeks ago I'd already sensed her presence up on the cliff top. It would have been consoling to know exactly what the future held, but I knew the folly of the speculation. 'If it is what God wants of you,' Father Christopher had advised me last year, 'then it will come about.' I'd been granted the leave of absence. I'd heard Thomas Merton: 'If we've been given the gift of recognising the ground of our being as love, give it to the world. Tell them, just by being what you are.'

At heart I knew the destination. Only the actual route remained obscure. We were approaching London. The motorway was lit here. Peter leaned forward from the back seat. 'We'll be there soon. Let's hope they've saved supper.' It was three months to the day that I'd made the journey in the opposite direction.

Chapter 10

I'D RETURNED TO AMBROSE AND MONICA. Although less tired owing to Nell's administrations, anxiety gripped me whenever I stopped to think. Landing myself on friends, however welcoming, only enhanced my worries. Predictably Ambrose and Monica never flinched; they simply gathered me into their circle as if I'd been orphaned. They introduced me to friends, who were kind and inquisitive. I wore clothes from Monica's wardrobe, others diverted from charity shops. 'My dear, we always buy clothes from Oxfam!' they announced. I tried on a woollen skirt in a shade of plum which barely reached my knees, wondering to whom it had belonged. There were also shirts and knitted jerseys. It was an odd sensation. In the community we had shared most things, but never garments. 'That colour really suits you,' they told me again and again.

I took the bus and went to see my Abbess. All the way there I pictured the scene in the convent parlour. I could imagine her greeting. 'There, dear,' she would probably say, 'I told you so. You should never have left us.' When she actually walked in she held out her arms.

'You must be absolutely exhausted,' she said as she hugged me. Compassion had replaced any strain between us. I gave her the doughnuts I'd bought for the community. She grinned. 'How delicious!' The polished wood floor, the utility chairs, the few out-of-date journals on the window sill were all exactly as I remembered them. Muted sunlight fell through the frosted window. At length we spoke of my future.

'You certainly had an unforeseen job awaiting you, dear,' she conceded, 'but I suspect not without precedent in the ways of God! His plans for us seldom coincide with our preconceived ideas – we only see the pattern with hindsight. I think you should take your remaining leave of absence. We'll pray the way becomes clear. I'm sure for the time being it's important you rest all you can.'

★

A week later the telephone rang. Ambrose came in from the hall. 'That was Felicity,' he said. 'She wonders if you would consider living in Hove until your leave is up. Her fiancé has an unoccupied furnished house a few doors away from her own and they'd love you to use this, if you are interested.'

Felicity was a friend of Elizabeth. She was distantly related to Basil. I'd met her for the first time at Elizabeth's funeral, when she'd come down from Hove, the Regency resort that runs along the Sussex coast from Brighton.

'Ambrose, I hardly know her!' I gasped. 'That's an amazingly generous offer.'

'If you're interested, she says we can take you over to see it and fix dates and so on. What do you think?'

I was astonished. I had prayed for guidance, but my prayers lacked assurance; I'd felt like a swimmer unable to take one toe off the bottom. I'd racked my brains trying to work out a practical direction for the eight months ahead. That this had come out of the blue left me reeling.

Ambrose poured glasses of sherry. Monica beamed. 'Here's to the next step, darling!' she toasted me. 'Of course we always knew you'd be shown the way!'

Her confidence had been greater than mine.

Ambrose took us to see Felicity. We parked outside her terrace of white-rendered villas, where sunlight reflected from windows and tiny front gardens looked bright with shrubs and a few late roses. Squabbling seagulls screamed abuse from chimneys and rooftops. We opened Felicity's wrought iron gate and climbed steps to the blue front door.

'Come in!' she greeted us. She welcomed Ambrose and Monica then held out her hand to me. 'Lovely to see you again – we've thought of you such a lot. The house was Stanley's idea.'

I knew Felicity had been a widow for several years; apparently Stanley's wife had died later. Since then they had fallen in love, planning to marry when possible. I'd never met Stanley. He came through now from another room and Felicity made introductions. Slightly built, he wore trousers of cavalry twill. A paisley silk square was tucked into his open-necked shirt and his shoes were as polished as Kate's coat. He must have been in his fifties. 'Come and look at the house!' he suggested, smiling broadly.

The house was on the other side of the street. Externally it looked identical to the rest of the Georgian villas. Stanley unlocked the front door. It was green, the brass knocker shaped like a dolphin. Entering, we found ourselves in a large sunny room out of which led a staircase. A green carpet stretched from wall to wall. Chairs, sofas, as well as antique furniture were placed elegantly about the room. Long curtains were of a William Morris design. I found myself laughing. 'I know God's ways are mysterious,' I giggled, 'but isn't this rather pushing the boat out?'

Stanley was happy. He led us to the kitchen at the back of the house, where every cupboard had louvered doors. Upstairs were two bedrooms and a bathroom. A basement ran the length of the house, storing various unused furniture.

'If you would care to occupy the house until your leave is up,' Stanley said, 'it would give us great pleasure. We don't want you to pay rent, simply your running expenses. We both feel we'd like to do this in memory of Elizabeth.'

I recalled Elizabeth's 'never worry' when she lay dying. I thought of my Abbess and her promise of prayers. As I looked at Stanley, I tried to marshal my words.

'I'm dumbstruck!' I stuttered, 'I can't begin to express my thanks. It would be wonderful to come here. Had you a date in mind?'

We settled for 24 September.

I telephoned Peter. 'Any chance of your coming this way before long?' I asked when I'd told him about the move. 'I could use my typewriter now, and there's room for the engraving tools – and my gumboots!'

The community was delighted. I thanked them, as ever, for their prayers. Sister St Richard offered me plants for the little front garden. I promised I'd let her know what might be needed. I wished I could show them the house.

Ambrose and Monica deposited me at eleven on the 24th. Stanley was there to hand over the door key. Ambrose and I carted Basil's tin trunk to the bedroom, Monica following with a large bag of groceries she'd produced. 'We'll be over to see you soon,' they promised, after coffee I'd made was finished. I saw them off down the road.

It was the first time I had been on my own. I walked through the house. I investigated cupboards lining the fitted kitchen. Many were stocked with basic ingredients, others with dishes and saucepans. Everything was immaculate. I thought of The Hollies. Elizabeth and I had never achieved our kitchen. I unpacked the groceries, grateful for Monica's generosity.

From a window above the sink I could see the extending backs of the terrace. A cat made its way along a dividing wall. He stepped gingerly, tail erect, concentrating as if he were walking a tightrope. Gulls still complained from the roof. As I contemplated the intricacies of the eye-level grill something within me sensed the start of another chapter. Silently I prayed, if it were, that events would prove less hazardous than the first.

Felicity took me to meet my near neighbour, Marcelle Bernstein. I knew her name because I'd read her book *Nuns* aloud in the refectory during community suppers. Felicity told me she had written several novels since then. Marcelle was interested and vivacious and asked me about the convent. She invited me to dinner. I found her easy to talk with and was happy to have a new friend. I was beginning to find my feet.

Felicity and Stanley

I discovered the priest at the parish church was one I knew. He had been appointed there only three weeks before. I saw him after Mass and he wanted to hear what had brought me away from the convent. He listened with sympathy. He was almost as incredulous as Madeleine in Penzance. 'You were certainly pushed in at the deep end!' he smiled. I asked his advice about my finances. Decisions were one of my greatest trials. Making them almost disabled me, as if they had tentacles. Since noviciate days 'giving up one's will' had been the hallmark of a vow of obedience. I could accept or obey with alacrity, but still felt guilt when left to a choice of my own. I wondered if I should apply for help from the social services. Father Terry was in favour. He thought it sensible, if only for a time.

The following Monday I called at the Social Security office. Rows of plastic seats filled the waiting room, racks held an array of leaflets. Waiting applicants sat staring vacantly, some read newspapers, one or two women had children with them. The room was not very clean. I sat with them until it was my turn for a cubicle, unsure what I might expect. From behind his grille the middle-aged interviewer required details of my finances. He looked grey and unwell. He asked if I had a P45, but I had no idea what he meant. He then wanted to know what work I was able to do. I hesitated to catalogue all we got through in the convent, but was inspired to mention my glass engraving. He'd never heard of this. He sighed. I devoutly hoped he was not about to expire. 'I'm sorry I'm giving you this trouble,' I apologised. He looked up at me with sad bloodshot eyes. 'You'll get a letter from us,' he said with measured patience, 'which will explain what help you can get.' As I thanked him I wished I could have made him a strong cup of tea. I rose from the uncomfortable stool, my place immediately taken by the next young man in the queue.

Three days later I had a letter, not from the DSS, but from a woman I'd met through Monica. 'Would you,' she wrote, 'consider giving the small group that meets in my house a talk on your recent experience, with your observation on life outside your community?' If I were willing, she ended, she would be only too happy to collect me on the first Tuesday afternoon of the month. Conditioned as always by years of obedience, I agreed to do what I could to help. I felt I owed that to Monica. Later, when the day came, I wondered why I'd been so obliging. I washed my hair in an effort to boost my confidence and tried to collect my thoughts. I also prayed.

Mrs Willis came promptly at two. She did everything to put me at ease, though without success. When we arrived at her bungalow she led me to a spacious room where ladies sat talking from deep armchairs. Mrs Willis signalled for silence. 'I know you will welcome Sister Giles,' she said. I wondered how she could be so certain. I tried to smile politely.

My mouth felt dry but I resisted the temptation to run from the room. I thanked them for their invitation. 'I must first of all tell you that I haven't "leapt over the wall",' I began. I felt my audience relax. I had taken the plunge. As I told of events that led to my going to The Hollies, it gradually became a little easier. I described Elizabeth's dying after our hopes for her recovery, followed so soon by Basil's death. I spoke of faith, and love such as Thomas Merton had described. 'Your whole life consists of burning bridges behind you,' I quoted from lines of his I suddenly remembered.

I blushed as my audience clapped. Mrs Willis said a few words of thanks, then someone called Mary came over with tea and iced cakes. The tea was essential. I was biting into a pink sugar cake when a grey-haired woman approached. Cup and saucer in hand, she said she'd been moved to hear of Elizabeth's courage in illness. 'I wonder if you'd allow me to come and talk to you one day? There's so much I'd like to discuss. My daughter, you see, has cancer.' A template had been made. Today a pattern had emerged that was to recur many times in the coming months and years.

Chapter 11

DAILY LIFE SETTLED. The man at the DSS had been true to his word, kindly putting through an allowance. Though restricted by this from earning more than a very small sum, I was able to type letters for the busy parish priest two mornings a week. I also met local parishioners at daily Mass.

Stanley and Felicity left me strictly to myself, not wishing to intrude on what they referred to as my way of life. Further invitations, stemming from Mrs Willis, came from house groups, others wrote asking if they could call. 'You know I'm not really a counsellor!' I protested as I listened. I resolved to master Stanley's fan-assisted oven in an effort to make cakes for their tea.

I met artist friends of Felicity who lived in the same street. Joanna was a niece of Dora Carrington. They spent six months of the year in France, returning in September. One day Felicity and I had lunch with them; they seldom stopped work, but today had laid down their brushes. Their kitchen was decorated in the style of Duncan Grant's at Charleston. We sat at a sea-green painted table laden with pottery bowls of salad, platters of meats, fresh bread, cheeses, anchovies and olives. We drank glasses of good French wine. I found myself reminded again of Madeleine.

John, a retired stockbroker whom I'd first met in the convent parlour, kept in touch. He was very devout; I suspected he was concerned for my soul. That I now appeared to have forsaken my recognisable vocation could be incomprehensible to him.

'I'd be delighted to give you lunch after Mass at Westminster Cathedral,' he wrote.

Two years earlier, I'd attended one of our consultative committee meetings in London, but that had been held at Farm Street. Last August I'd stayed overnight at the house of Peter's brother-in-law when we came from North Devon, but that hardly counted. It was a long time since I'd visited Westminster Cathedral. A cheap day return from Brighton was tempting. I thought I might try it.

'I'd love to come to London,' I answered when I'd checked about trains. His postcard confirmed that he'd be waiting at W.H. Smith on the station's concourse.

I wore Monica's shirtwaister safari style dress. It was tight, but not uncomfortable, the belt on the furthest hole. Felicity had given me my shoes; I'd already bought a small handbag. The train was on time and I spotted John as I walked through from the barrier. He had not seen me without my habit. I saw a flicker of disbelief before his usual courteous greeting.

'My dear, how good to see you,' he smiled, 'I'd forgotten you would be out of your habit!'

We walked to the cathedral, exchanging news politely whilst we worked our way through crowded crossings at traffic lights. I had never seen the piazza; it had been completed sometime after I'd entered the convent. 'I've seen photographs, but how lovely to see the real thing!' I exclaimed like a tourist.

We entered the cathedral. John took holy water, making the sign of the cross. I followed. Visitors and worshippers mingled inside the great doors; someone scraped a chair, the sound echoing through the lofty nave. Then John led me down towards the high altar. Near the front, he genuflected, waiting as I did the same. I took the seat he indicated, putting my handbag on the floor in front of me before I knelt. Above the altar, prepared for Mass, shafted light fell from the cupola windows, faintly purple on incense-laden air. A bell rang and a procession of servers preceded the vested priest to the sanctuary. We all stood. When they reached the high altar the celebrant's voice came clearly over the microphone. 'In the name of the Father, and of the Son, and of the Holy Spirit.' In Westminster Cathedral or the smallest country parish, the words of Mass were the same. Byzantine mosaics, gilding, stone reliefs, side chapels, could never change the significance of the Word of God. With John, I stood or knelt, one among hundreds, in communion not only with each other, but with God who created us.

'Through him, with him, in him, in the unity of the Holy Spirit all honour and glory is yours, almighty Father, for ever and ever.'

'Amen,' we replied resoundingly.

When Mass was over John took me to a small Italian restaurant. As we walked in, a waiter, recognising him, came forward. He showed us to a table near the window. Tablecloths and napkins were pink. John ordered *sformato di tagliatelle*, which sounded more exciting than macaroni cheese in the convent. We drank chilled Frascati, which John decided I should like. I was thirsty; it tasted delicious.

'Now,' he said, as I helped myself to a crusty roll. 'Tell me your plans – how do you see your life evolving? I expect you have written yourself some sort of schedule? What time limit have you set? A good general must have a strategy! I'm sure you have something in mind . . .'

'John,' I confessed. 'I haven't any plans!' I felt exposed, as if I were at a community chapter meeting. 'I believe the whole point is in *not* having them. I'm coming to realise that I must live each day in faith as it comes – to be free, available when needed.' I sounded like a remnant from the sixties, a 'traveller', with lurcher and broken down vehicle. How could I explain that I was coming to see my vocation as an outcome of prayer duly practised, an attitude of acceptance, requiring adaptability to each day's events? 'Here I am, Lord, I come to do your will,' sounded relevant in the fortieth psalm. From me, living off charity, I could see the discrepancy.

John was a kind man. His desire to be helpful was genuine. He put down his glass. 'I suggest you compose a set of rules for yourself,' he said. 'Give me something in writing, a project – anything I can use towards the raising of funds.'

I sensed the disappointment I was. Even the lipstick I'd worn had been lost to the tagliatelle. John would have liked me to become a success, the force behind a new venture with which he too could be associated. I could think of nothing positive to contribute. 'I'm sorry I'm so undynamic!' was all I could manage. We took a taxi back to Victoria. He bought me chrysanthemums, kissing me lightly on the cheek as we said goodbye.

'Thank you for lunch, John,' I said, genuinely grateful.

He smiled down at me. 'I meant what I said about wishing to help,' he told me. 'Work out your aims! I promise to keep in touch.' I knew he would. The thought of it pursued me all the way down in the train.

When I reached the house I found a letter waiting from my Abbess. By this time there were only two more months of my leave. I'd visited the community regularly, keeping her informed of the way my leave of absence had evolved. She agreed I might now seek a renewal of this, which Father Austin, she said, was kindly prepared to grant.

I hammered the stems of the chrysanthemums with swift elation. I'd never expected so encouraging a confirmation of my present state. Like a calf let out from its winter byre, I felt a sudden unimagined release. That I needed the community behind me, I hadn't the slightest doubt, but the underlying conviction that I must remain free was compelling. I wrote at once with my thanks. The renewal meant the end of my stay in Hove. Only now was I able to realise the extent of Stanley's kindness. During these few months in his house I had found a sense of independence, a slow emergence into a world beyond community enclosure or the unsought confinement of The Hollies. Sometimes I'd felt engulfed by a sense of unreality, as if transfixed between one world and another. Years of communal living had left an indelible imprint. I was punctilious over time. I woke swiftly at 5 a.m. ready to leap from bed at the sound of an imaginary bell. It was a surprise that my habit wasn't inside-out and ready to fling over my head, as it had been each morning in my community cell. But now, little by little, I'd schooled myself to a secular life, at the same time loath to cut threads that bound me to my consecration. I'd met people who came to discuss their difficulties, but from whom I had also gained greatly. Felicity had been a link with Elizabeth, sharing with me memories of happier days, helping me understand another side of Elizabeth's personality. Above all I'd begun to sense the direction, however undefined, in which my vocation lay.

In the April, I took a train to Littlehampton, a half-hour's journey, to visit an elderly friend. Harriet lived in a flat overlooking the sea. Long known to my family, she'd been a regular visitor at the convent, intelligent, amusing, always interested, except when affected by bouts of the depressive illness which dogged her in later life. She always referred to the community as The Brigade of Guards. Now in her eighties, never having had to boil an egg for herself, she was looked after by a self-effacing housekeeper. She'd spent her youth in Paris, entertaining for her father in the British Embassy. She also held a highly esteemed French medal for her gallantry during the second world war. It was almost a year since I'd seen her.

'Can't you come over here?' she suggested, when I told her I must find somewhere to live. We were drinking coffee from French porcelain cups.

'Have you anything to rent?' I asked.

'There's the flat next door!' she said. 'Liz and Jim own the house and are looking for a tenant to take the ground floor – I'll ring them!'

Half an hour later we were inspecting the flat.

Less elegantly furnished than Stanley's house, its character was nonetheless charming. Sitting room and bedroom led through to a dining room at the back, with kitchen and bathroom beyond. There was even a tiny conservatory. The owners, who lived in London, used the house for weekends and holidays. Their hope was for someone to occupy the ground floor on a long term let. The rent was nominal.

'It's obviously intended for you!' encouraged Harriet. Liz and Jim, not averse to a gamble, agreed.

'We'll have it ready by 1 May – would that suit you? We'll get you to sign the agreement when you arrive.'

The decision, I felt, was out of my hands. I needed a place to live. With a flat unexpectedly placed in my lap, who was I to refuse? 'Thank you,' I whispered, as I sat once more on the train. 'I will keep thee full surely,' I remembered from Julian of Norwich.

A few days later I heard from Sister Ignatius. Over the years we'd corresponded, her community enclosed like my own. She had only recently heard of my leave of absence. She was very upset. 'How could you do this?' she wrote. 'Had you forgotten your contemplative vocation? A religious sister is no longer at liberty in the world! Surely what they tell me cannot be true!' She then quoted Gray:

Full many a flower is born to blush unseen,
And waste its sweetness on the desert air.

I was unsure how I was going to reply to that.

Chapter 12

I ARRIVED IN LITTLEHAMPTON ON 1 May, bags and trunks conveyed as ever by Ambrose. He and Monica lived only a few miles away. 'Getting accustomed to this!' Ambrose teased. Monica once more produced groceries. She also bought flowers, blue irises and pheasant-eye narcissi. I arranged them on a low table which stood in the window bay.

It hadn't taken long to feel I had lived there for years. The flat had a holiday atmosphere; buckets, spades and shrimping nets might not be apparent, but the hall was redolent of sandy mornings by the sea.

I met neighbours. One couple was beset by marital difficulties and I found myself precipitated into their agony. Sometimes their arguments shattered my silence; frequently they would come to the flat individually, wanting someone to listen. I did what I could, praying for both of them. Mass was held at a nearby convent school, the sisters there becoming friends. They asked if I'd coach two Spanish sisters in English. That the two did eventually manage a phrase in English was certainly no credit to me. People invited me to coffee, or sometimes tea. I found myself busy, beginning to be recognised in the street. 'Hello, Sister!' I'd be greeted as I grinned in reply. The greengrocer presented me with grapefruit or an extra apple or two.

Harriet had become too old to drive. 'They won't renew my licence!' she fumed. She offered me her Toyota. I laughed. 'That's my second chance of a car!' I told her, remembering Elizabeth's Beetle.

'You see! You're meant to have one,' said Harriet. 'You'd better take a few lessons before your test!'

She said she would pay for these. At my first lesson, the instructor suggested I get more practice. The three-point turn had taken at least sixteen. I asked Monica to pray. Later, she came with me to the test centre, waiting whilst I went through the required manoeuvres. 'What are the white lights used for at the rear of the car?' interrogated the examiner as we drew towards the end of my test. I hadn't the slightest idea. The only car I had driven before entering the convent had been my Austin Seven. I felt myself begin to go pink. 'In what situation do you need illumination behind you?' urged the examiner. 'Please think. I'm trying to help you.'

I was paralysed with anxiety. Only after immense effort the answer suddenly dawned. 'To reverse!' I squawked, just in the nick of time. I passed the test. Harriet was delighted when I was able to tell her. In the last three weeks she'd suffered another bout of depression, returning to hospital in London for radical treatment. As soon as I felt confident enough I drove there to see her. 'Well done!' she managed to smile. She asked me to drive her round Richmond Park. I took her for the first of many drives, with half an hour spent in the peace of the Isabella Plantation before taking her back to the hospital.

Sister St Richard was elected Abbess of the community. Elections were held every three years, an abbess seldom in office longer than six. She had always done everything possible to ease my path; now she rang regularly, making sure all was well. She ordered clothes for me from catalogues sent to the convent and made certain there were eggs or vegetables if I visited the community. Their cabbage tasted better than the sea spinach I illegally picked along the beach. In September she was due to visit a sister community in Devon. 'I wondered,' she said on the telephone, 'what you would say to a few days' holiday, taking the car? I should pay our costs.'

The diocese had kindly allotted me £5000. Invested by them the interest provided my income. I was torn between tying myself to regular employment or remaining available for those in need. I'd taken the latter course, but the income did not stretch to the rent. For that I had still to rely on the DSS.

At seven-thirty on Monday morning I arrived at the convent main door. Sister St Richard was waiting. 'You start loading the car,' she called, disappearing into the passage. 'I shan't be a jiff.'

The porch was piled with bags and cartons. History was repeating itself. Sister St Richard re-appeared with a large box of kindling. 'But we're only away for three days,' I reminded her, having difficulty packing the boot. 'I know,' she said, 'but those tins will save us paying out money on food – the kindling will save us collecting all that damp driftwood.'

She had permission to stay two nights in a cottage her family owned on the Somerset coast. She was determined it would be fun.

What I was unable to stow in the boot I stacked on the back seat of the car. A thermos containing milk for the coffee sat in a basket with plastic beakers and parcels of corned beef sandwiches. The corned beef was a concession. Normally we had never partaken of meat. When we were both installed, I started the engine and let in the clutch. We moved slowly down the drive, but not more than fifty yards. 'Hang on! I've forgotten the geraniums!' she exclaimed. Ten minutes later we set off again. The geraniums, some with canes to support them, stood between bags and baskets in the well of the car. My view from the rear window was vertically obstructed by bamboo.

'Why do we need geraniums?' I enquired edgily.

'They're to leave at the cottage for Guy,' she said. 'I promised I'd let him have cuttings.'

'Those are no longer cuttings!' I argued. 'They're fully grown trees!'

'Well, I know,' conceded Sister St Richard. 'But I thought as we'd got the car . . .'

Activities were greatly extended by the car. I took members of the community to dentist or hospital if required. The radius was widened for talks or visiting. One day I was asked to call at the hospice where someone's father lay dying. Within half an hour I was sitting beside him, thankful to draw on all I'd learned from Elizabeth's illness, trying to give him peace. I saw him gradually relax as I sat there. Two hours after I'd left he died, slipping away in his sleep.

One morning I took the car to Hove. I wanted to see Father Terry, the priest who had always looked after my affairs, spiritual help backed by sound practical advice. Once I had parked, I crossed the wide road on my way to the church. I was nearly hit by a car. When it drew into the kerb beyond me, I walked over to apologise to the driver. 'I'm so sorry,' I said, 'I was preoccupied and never saw you coming.'

The woman eased herself from the car. Her hair was tinted a reddish brown. 'I shouldn't really be driving today,' she said. 'It's the anniversary of my husband's death. I miss him dreadfully.'

We walked along the pavement together. She had a coat over her arm which she said she was taking to be cleaned.

'I can guess your pain,' I said.

'Are you a widow?'

'No. Actually I'm a nun!' It sounded unlikely. I wore a summer skirt and a touch of eyeshadow.

'You're not! I never met a nun before. I'm Jewish. I used to believe – not any more, my faith's gone.'

We stood on the corner of Western Road discussing life after death. I had no desire to thrust my belief at her, nor dilute her personal grief, I simply wished to console. 'Love might be painful, it's never wasted, never lost,' I added. There were tears in her eyes. Her hand as she took mine had scarlet tipped fingers.

'I'm glad I nearly ran you down!' she managed to smile. 'You'll pray for Zach, won't you?'

'Of course,' I promised.

Nell came to stay a night. I gave her my bed and slept on the sitting room divan. She'd loaded her car with things for the flat, including an electric blanket for winter. She also brought a begonia. 'That plant won first prize in the flower show!' she boasted as I admired it. We spoke of the village, of Peter and Dr Hughes. She brought her own bottle of whisky, recalling vividly evenings at The Hollies with Basil. When she went, she gave me a cheque. 'Buy yourself a washing machine, darling!' she told me. 'It will be an enormous help. I'm giving it now instead of leaving you money in my will!' I promised to visit her in the spring if I possibly could.

A sister from the local convent asked if I'd give a talk on the subject of prayer at the open prison. I was aghast. 'I'd die with fright!' I said. She worked there herself, much valued by prisoners and staff, but I knew my own limitations. 'You can do it!' she insisted, refusing to take my excuses. Still doubtful, I eventually surrendered.

I tried to prepare words. I rang Sister St Richard, begging prayers. All the way to the prison I reminded myself of the analogy I'd so often quoted. 'Keep the hosepipe unblocked!' I pleaded repeatedly as I drove. 'Keep ME out of the way. Let it be YOUR words in me . . .'

I arrived at the prison gates. The guard, expecting me, let me through. I walked to the chapel. As I entered, my eye was caught by a blackboard, a notice there scribbled in chalk.

'SISTER GILES IS SPEAKING IN THE CHAPEL AT 6.30 THIS EVENING. BE SURE YOU ARE THERE.' Beneath this was added, in another hand, 'ESCAPING FROM THE MAFIA IS EASIER THAN GETTING OUT OF AN ENCLOSED CONVENT, DON'T MISS.'

Even in my terror I laughed. The chaplain came forward to greet me. I was led to the sanctuary where a seat had been placed before the altar. Benches were filled with men in striped shirts, their eyes upon me. Somehow I rose to my feet. 'I'm not sure about the Mafia,' I began, 'but I'd like you to know that I've been "inside" a great deal longer than any of you!'

They took my point. They laughed. I went on to tell them of God's abiding love for us, that enclosure, voluntary or in their case compulsory, need be no impediment to the practice of prayer – sometimes even an advantage. I told them of life in a convent, of the privilege it was to pray for others. I never dried up. Sentence after sentence flashed like teletext into my head. The prayers I'd urgently asked of the community were tangible. At length I drew to a close. I invited questions. A prisoner, sitting in the front pew, shot up his hand; he was black, his large eyes expressive.

'Sister,' he said, 'you speak of Love – now what do you say when the person you love don' love you?'

I guessed he had lost his girl.

'I'm afraid this is probably the result of whatever you did that made you fetch up here,' I suggested, 'but have you thought of the love Jesus had for us all? He loved so much that he allowed himself to be nailed to the Cross for it. That love really was excruciating, yet look how he redeemed the world by his pain. You too can use your love in that way! Try asking that it may help the person you love – then your love, the real love, will never be lost –'

'Sister –' he nodded slowly '– I never did think of that.'

They then begged me to stay till their time was up. I joined them for prayers, led by themselves.

Driving home, I glanced at a bunch of bright dahlias beside me. I could scarcely believe the evening was over. As with those who came to the flat to talk, it was always I who gained. As I changed gear for the corner, I little thought that prisoners would mark the first of such days of prayer. In the ways of initiation this one was unlikely to be repeated. Future days would take place in parish churches, or sometimes in private homes.

Chapter 13

THE PROVINCIAL OF THE ORDER wrote asking me to visit him. He was staying in the local convent, recuperating from illness. I had known him from his meetings with the community; he knew of my own circumstances through Father Austin when he granted my leave.

I called the following Thursday. The convent was also a rest home; elderly patients in varying stages of disability reclined in the vestibule. A passing sister directed me to Father Provincial's room. 'Come in,' he called quietly as I tapped on his door. He rose to greet me; I'd forgotten how kind a face he had. Another sister brought coffee. He handed me a cup and sat back in his chair stirring his own.

'I think the time has come for you to obtain a dispensation from your vows,' he said, without preamble. 'It is not really satisfactory renewing your leave like this. From what I hear it seems obvious you are leading a life that is right for you, that God called you to care for your friend in North Devon. You were his instrument for bringing her into the Church. That he brought you from the enclosure to do so must be regarded as part of his providence, but I think you must now regularise your position.'

My heart sank. Father Provincial was a canon lawyer. Despite his frailty, there was no diminution of his mental faculties. 'What should I do?' I asked, dreading a severance from the community.

'There is a newly revised edition of the Code of Canon Law,' he said. 'It was published a few years ago. Canon 604, I think, should cover your position. You would remain consecrated, yet released from community life.' The possibility of renewed consecration was a straw at which I could clutch. He told me I must write to Rome requesting a dispensation. I had no idea how to word this and asked him for help. After a formal opening I jotted down his lines: 'Having had a leave of absence for three years to live a consecrated life outside the enclosure, and with the wholehearted desire of remaining consecrated to God, I beg this dispensation so that I may continue a way of life to which I have felt called – that is, to live according to

Canon 604 of the new Code of Canon Law – which I realise is incompatible with the life of canonical enclosure.'

I thanked Father Provincial. I realised he'd only done what he knew to be right, yet he had taken trouble to ensure I was let down lightly. 'Tell me how you get on,' he said, before giving his blessing. He walked with me to the door. Outside, I found myself shaking. I walked back to the flat scarcely noticing where I was going. The step I was about to take was irreversible; never in all my years in the community had I considered a formal separation. My hope had been that this leave of absence might become an acceptable extension of my original vocation. Now I was being forced to choose between one way of life or another – I felt shattered.

It took me an agonising three days to make the choice. Eventually, in my heart I knew there was none to make.

The Bishop said I might renew my vows in the convent chapel. In his absence, Sister St Richard was delegated to receive them. We chose 25 March for the small ceremony.

Father Tony celebrated the Mass. After he'd read the Gospel, he gave a short address. 'The years of enclosure have been a training,' he said, 'an invaluable structure on which you will continually depend.' He then called me to the altar steps, where I knelt while he read the opening prayer from the rite of consecration. 'Never forget that you are given over entirely to the service of the Church and of all your brothers and sisters. You are an apostle in the Church and in the world, in the things of the Spirit and in the things of the world. Let your light, then, shine before men and women, that your Father in heaven may be glorified, and his plan for making all things one in Christ, come to perfection. Love everyone, especially those in need. Help the poor, care for the weak, teach the ignorant, protect the young, minister to the old, bring strength and comfort to widows and all in adversity.'

Sister St Richard came forward to receive my vows. I placed my hands in hers, reciting the promise of consecration. I also vowed to live in the spirit of Saint Francis and particularly of my former community, which meant so much to me. My ring of profession, removed from my finger and cleaned, lay with my breviary in a basket beside the altar. Sister St Richard fetched these, handing them back to me as part of the consecration rite.

Mass continued, a solemn celebration of the feast of the Annunciation. 'May we celebrate with joy today this sacrament of your love,'

I heard Father Tony pray over the bread and wine. Afterwards the community gave me cards they had signed, Sister St Richard beaming as if I'd just become a newly clothed novice. I felt I belonged again. Relationship with the community, though subtly changed, to my immense relief was restored.

Days lengthened. Easter came, daffodils were everywhere. In May I was invited to help with handicapped pilgrims in Lourdes, the pilgrimage run by the ecclesiastical Knights of Malta. I remembered the long black habits I'd made for them in the convent vestment room. In Lourdes these were worn only occasionally. Women were issued with white nurses' dresses and aprons, reminiscent of 1914. VAD head veils enhanced the impression. Physical suffering, faith, spiritual grace, and the worst of trinkets displayed in every visible tight-packed shop, summed up my first impression of Lourdes. Our sick pilgrims were housed in the 'Sept Douleurs' hospice, hardly updated, I felt, since its institution. We worked in teams, dressing, washing, feeding and wheeling our pilgrims to every place of devotion. We took them to the grotto where Bernadette had her visions of Our Lady; we pushed their chairs in the torchlight procession, with thousands singing the Lourdes hymn, candles guttering in the evening breeze despite paper cups protecting them; we made our way through narrow streets where nationalities seemed more diverse than flowers in an alpine meadow.

Sandy, one of the pilgrims, had recently developed multiple sclerosis. She longed to bathe in the holy waters of Lourdes. On the third afternoon I accompanied her to the low building where the baths were housed beside the grotto. We waited with many others, sitting on benches until we were called. It was a solemn ritual. Shepherded to cubicles, six at a time, we undressed in silence, exchanging our clothes for the thin cotton cloak we were given. In due course a helper in charge summoned us to the actual bath. I wondered whether we should be told how to take it. I needn't have worried. When my turn came, two attendants stood like guardians, deftly removing the cotton cloak as they substituted it for an already wet capacious garment. To the recitation of prayers, I was guided down steps to the stone bath, eased back into the water and out again immediately. The wet cloak was removed, the cotton one replaced, and I was returned to the cubicle to retrieve my clothes. I could hardly believe it was over. Sandy had now taken my place in the queue. She could walk with the help of a stick, if a little unsteadily. By the time she came to the cubicle again, I was half clad. Her broad smile almost enveloped me, speech inhibited only by the silence we were obliged to observe. I helped her dress and together we walked out to the warm sunshine. Benches were still full, wheelchairs drawn up alongside. I wondered how many passed through the baths each day.

'I've been longing for that holy bath.' Sandy smiled happily. 'I don't mind if it doesn't physically heal me – it's the feeling of joy it gives! They said you receive grace from Our Lady. I believe that! I'm GLOWING!'

Late that evening I made my way back to the grotto. We'd fed our sick pilgrims, helping them to bed in their dormitory. Father Philip had taken night prayers. I was free. Great candles burned before the shrine in a forest of light. The Gave ran quietly beyond the low parapet behind me. I knelt on the warm ground. 'Give me Sandy's faith,' I prayed. 'Help me with your grace to walk the path of my vocation. Be in me the love I long to give.'

It was almost midnight when I turned from the grotto. Untold hosts of stars punctured the darkness. I walked slowly past the Basilica, crossing the great square now nearly empty. Up in the town people were still sitting outside cafés, talking with friends, drinking, laughing. A waiter, tray in hand, placed cups of cappuccino on a table as I passed. Shops were still open, plastic souvenirs strung like onions in their windows. From one of the churches I heard a clock chime. It pealed out the Lourdes hymn to mark the hour: '*Ave, ave, ave, Maria.*' In six hours' time I'd be on duty again.

Later that September, I was reminded of Sandy's joy. I'd decided to walk home along the shore after a day in London. The tide was out almost a mile, revealing firm wet sand. Removing my shoes, I noticed a woman, the only person in sight, doing the same. Together we picked our way, shoes in hand, across the shingle. I slung my bag over my shoulder.

'Phew!' grinned the woman, 'Just what I was longing for! Cool wet sand! I work in an old people's home – come down here on my weekend off – it sets me up.'

'Doing that for me as well!' I agreed.

We walked on, leaving slight imprints on the sand. The woman suddenly bent down. 'Look at that bit of pink seaweed!' she exclaimed. Merely a thread, it was caught on a ridge where the tide had left the suspicion of a puddle. She straightened up. 'Now that really makes me happy inside.' The joy not only tangible in Lourdes, I thought. 'Be still and know that I am God' was just as apt on the shore at Littlehampton. 'I feel like that too!' I smiled. We reached the groyne where the cormorant habitually perched, wings extended as if he were a lectern. 'This is where I climb the beach again,' I said. She said she'd come with me. We replaced our shoes, crawling our way up steep shingle to the sea road. Our ways diverged.

' 'Bye,' she waved, 'must be back for my crab salad now! Wouldn't miss crab for tea in the boarding house!'

I turned in at the flat. It felt strangely musty after the sea air. Evening sun picked out the fly marks on the closed sash windows. I walked across to open one.

The following spring Nick's wife gave birth to a son, their third child. She asked if I would act as godmother. 'His name is Christopher,' she told me. They placed him in my arms and I kissed his downy head, smooth and warm. His tiny fists were clenched against his shawl. 'I'll keep an eye on you,' I whispered, uncertain whether I spoke to him or to Elizabeth.

Nick invited Peter to be his godfather.

Mary was to marry Anthony at the end of May. Her grandfather, the XVth Duke of Norfolk, had provided the land on which the convent was built; his wife, Duchess Flora, had sold her jewels to provide for the building itself. The Community had been founded in 1886 at the request of the Duchess. She had earnestly desired prayers for her young invalid son. She herself died aged only thirty-two the following year, but the Norfolk family maintained a tradition of friendship as well as generosity throughout the years. Mary had known the community all her life. Since my coming to Littlehampton she had been in touch again. One morning in early January I answered the telephone and heard her voice.

'We're hoping to refurbish three adjoining cottages on the estate,' she told me. 'Amazingly, they have all become vacant together. Anthony and I plan to live in one of them – what would you feel about living next door?'

I was speechless.

'Come and see it!' Mary encouraged me. 'It would make a base for your work! Of course, though, you might not like it,' she added typically.

They took me to inspect the cottage. Uniformly overcast, the clouded sky could not obscure the panoramic view. Sussex flint buildings looked over water meadows to the river. Beyond it, wooded hills reached high to the south and west. Downland rose gently from behind the cottages. 'It's glorious . . .' I murmured in a daze.

The cottage was in need of repair. Workmen were already there. They hoped it would be ready by July. 'Could you see yourself here?' asked Mary.

They told me it would be rent-free.

Right from the start I had been provided for ceaselessly: Ambrose and Monica, Nell, Felicity and Stanley, the diocesan grant, cars, the goodness of friends – and now a cottage in perfect surroundings. I thought of John's insistence that I plan my life. No plan of mine could have incorporated this.

'It feels totally right,' I assured Mary.

Anthony smiled.

Lady Mary Mumford who gave me the rent-free cottage

'Home, not merely a base!' I told them.

One slight query however, shadowed my euphoria, but I kept it to myself. I actually had no furniture.

Three weeks later I opened my post. From a long envelope I extracted a letter. It came from a firm of solicitors. 'We act for the estate of the above deceased,' it stated. I read further. Enclosed was a legacy in the form of a cheque, from Harriet, who had died six months before. It was easily enough to buy basic furniture for the cottage. I gasped, regarding the cheque with disbelief. It never failed to amaze me that initial steps in the dark seemed almost a prerequisite of faith.

Liz and Jim were understanding. 'Of course you must accept,' they agreed. I called on the DSS, thanking them for having sponsored my rent at the flat. 'I'll be all right now,' I explained. 'I've been offered a rent-free cottage!' The girl remained concerned. 'You can always let us know if you ever need further assistance,' she said kindly.

I began the search for furniture. I picked up old kitchen chairs, stripping their chipped green paint until the original wood was revealed. I bought a power drill so that sanding and polishing would be easier. In a large electrical store I chose a brand new cooker as well as a fridge-freezer, and from an interior decorating shop bought yards of fabric in the sale, making curtains which I interlined with my calico convent sheets. Ambrose provided an armchair from their loft, and a nursing chair used by Monica when the children were young. Sister St Richard offered surplus crockery. Only the bedroom furniture had to come from the 'do-it-yourself' firm, packages strewn over the floor as I slotted together innumerable panels, retrieving screws that were never near when needed. The foreman at the cottage knew a carpet wholesaler. He took me to the warehouse where we met the manager. The smell of carpet bales was overpowering. The manager pointed out those he thought suitable for my stone floors.

'This one I'd advise,' he said, unrolling acres of pale green carpet. He told me the price. It took a while to do sums; the cost was more than I'd expected. This sort of expenditure was unfamiliar.

'It has a guarantee,' the man said. 'You won't be disappointed with the wear.' I hoped he was honest.

'All right,' I told him. 'I'd like it laid by the middle of June.'

The refurbished cottage was taking shape. I asked Pete, the foreman of the building firm, if two small living rooms might be turned into one. He also made the upstairs landing into an extra lavatory. The bathroom was downstairs. Suddenly the dining room shone with magnolia emulsion, the kitchen boasted a new sink and white fitted units. 'Where would you like the electricity points?' asked Ron the electrician.

The move was arranged for 1 July. 'Can you recommend a removal firm, Pete?' I asked.

'You're not having a firm,' he retorted, 'you're having us! The lads and I are going to bring your stuff over.'

The men arrived at seven-fifteen on the Sunday morning. They came with three open trucks and two transit vans. 'Here we are then!' grinned Bill. They set about removing cartons I'd stacked in the flat, then the chests and chairs, two beds, the bicycle that had belonged to Stanley's late wife, the table and an old kitchen trolley I thought might be useful. Bill lashed the unwieldy items on to his truck. 'Lucky it's not raining!' he said cheerfully.

I'd already said goodbye to friends and neighbours, settled any outstanding rent with Liz and Jim. Their flat had been an appreciated place of transition. I hoped they realised my gratitude. I carried what remained of the smaller items out to the car, locking the flat before posting the key through the letter box. 'We're off!' I called to Pete, as the men started up their engines. I glanced towards the flats on the other side of the square. Net curtains had been furtively lifted, interest in my departure roused by its singularity. In front of me I saw thin kitchen table legs astride a mattress on Bill's truck. Against an upended chair the garden rake lay where it had fallen, like some discarded lance. The convoy pulled away from Littlehampton. It took only half an hour to reach the cottage.

The valley, as we came down the hill, lay brightly green in the morning sun, the river almost motionless with reflected light. Chickens scattered as we turned in at the narrow lane, trees and bushes arched as a cathedral nave. Honeysuckle and a few late wayside roses struggled towards the sun.

Outside the cottage there was ample space for parking trucks and vans. Pete took charge of the unloading. Everything inside looked new, carpet stretching even to the cupboard under the stairs. The kitchen was in working order, power points exactly where needed.

'Pete, it's lovely,' I congratulated him as I filled the kettle. The men carted furniture, labelled to help them place it, glad to find the cottage cool after the heat outside. I hung the curtains. Bill, boasting a Mexican straw hat, rewound his rope and flung it into the empty truck. I mentioned payment.

'Don't you think about it!' Pete said. 'We enjoyed that!' added Bill. One of the others said they'd come over later to see how I'd settled in.

'I invite you all to a buffet lunch next week!' I compromised. I knew Mary and Anthony would not be coming till September. I should see the men frequently as they worked next door. The cottage on the further side had much yet to be done. I planned to provide their tea and coffee breaks whenever I could.

The next few days produced a heatwave; darkly tanned torsos worked from ladders, everyone sweltered. I drove to Chichester for cold meats, sausage rolls, flans and cheesecake towards the buffet lunch. I bought bottles of beer and Coke, and cream to go with the strawberries. They were a great success.

'I want to thank you,' I began as glasses at last were drained. 'I shall never forget your kindness. If I can ever be of help to any of you, I hope you will always come.'

'Thanks for a lovely lunch,' smiled Pete, shaking my hand.

A fortnight later Father Francis came to bless the cottage. 'May it be a place of peace for all who come,' he prayed as he walked from room to room with holy water. That evening I opened my breviary at the wrong place. A card I'd printed in the convent years ago marked the page. The quotation was from the Flemish mystic, Ruysbroeck. 'The love of God is an inflowing and an outpouring tide,' I read. People called, wishing to see my new surroundings. I was asked to give more talks. BBC Radio Sussex wrote inviting me to broadcast their Prayer for the Day for a week. The telephone rang a great deal. 'Any chance of a few days in your spare room?' a religious sister wrote from London. She'd just returned from duty in Pakistan. Everyone found solace in the quiet countryside. Groups met in the cottage for prayer, Father Francis offered Mass each month in the dining room. I was rung up by people I did not know, who had been given my name by friends. 'May I come to see you?' they asked, often in distress, sometimes because they wanted advice about a possible vocation. Others sought instruction before being received into the Church. I began an onslaught on the garden. Sister St Richard divided plants from the convent, heaving surplus shrubs or roses to the parlour in huge unwieldy boxes. I begged manure from the farm. Each morning and evening waves of wild geese flew over, distant honking a prelude to the precision of their flight. Peter came up from Devon.

'Strange how it's all come about,' he said. 'You thought it would be North Devon and The Hollies – it turned out to be Sussex and this place.'

He was right. I'd always remained aware of Elizabeth, of our initial intention. Everything had taken longer than expected, but I'd needed the intervening years to adapt. Uncertainty too had played a vital part. Without it, I could see, there would have been no need for faith, that underlying witness to God's providence and love. Now, at last, I'd been given exactly the right environment for working as Elizabeth and I had originally envisaged. It made me happy to my finger tips.

Chapter 14

Sister St Richard telephoned from the convent: 'I've gone down with shingles,' she told me. 'The community were wondering – now that you have the spare room – whether you might have me to stay till I get over the worst of it? I have permission to ask you.'

My hesitation was merely an indrawn breath. 'Of course,' I managed. 'When?'

I picked her up the following morning. The tiny cottage had by now taken shape. Further chairs, a larger table and a court-cupboard re-vamped from genuine seventeenth century oak in Victorian times, lent an air of stability to the dining-room. A framed print of Giotto's 'St Francis Feeding the Birds', presented by Ambrose, accentuated this. Making up the bed in the small spare bedroom, I recalled the preparation for Elizabeth's homecoming at The Hollies. No need this time for disinfectant. The cottage had been perfectly decorated throughout. I lined the drawers of the do-it-yourself chest, and picked wild scabious and campion from the lane to place on its surface. I hung my small crucifix above the bed.

Sister St Richard's shingles had affected her face. The rash was beginning to subside but the pain was intense, making her feel sick. I helped her up the short staircase and gingerly exchanged her habit for the voluminous white cotton nightgown she produced from her rucksack. At last she sank back on the pillows. I returned to the car. Even in her illness she had managed to accumulate an astonishing assortment of everything she considered essential: cartons, the thumb-stick she took whenever she left the convent, several bin liners and a white plastic bucket securely tied with garden twine, a label attached stating: THIS WAY UP. MEDICINES. IMPORTANT. Thankfully there were no geranium cuttings.

Once all had been accounted for and unpacked, I took her a bowl of soup I'd made from vegetables grown in Mary and Anthony's kitchen garden. Newly married, Mark and Julie had moved into the further cottage that April, Julie to work in the house for Mary whilst Mark, with a job of his own, had charge of the vegetables. Runner beans, leeks and carrots – and in the greenhouse tomatoes and cucumbers – were a continual source of my sustenance.

Sister St Richard managed the soup, and I administered pills and lotions unearthed from the plastic bucket. I settled her down to rest, a large cowbell by her side so that she could summon me if needed. Several books, brought from the convent library, remained unopened, waiting for when she felt able to read. Over the next few days I watched her relax and slowly regain her appetite. She told me she dearly wished for a bath. The following morning we thought we might attempt this. Still shaky, she asked me to hang on as she lowered herself into the warm soapy water. As I left her to wallow, I remembered the galvanised tin baths kept beneath our beds when I first entered the convent. There were no bathrooms then and once, on Christmas Eve, I thought I would treat myself to the primitive luxury. I'd filled the oval bath with two pails of hot water drawn from a downstairs kitchen tap. Savouring the moment, I'd drawn off my habit, then the 'chemise' made from a thick woollen fabric reminiscent of a tennis ball, and finally the ample calico 'ducks' we wore for knickers. Naked, I'd stepped into the tin bath, drawing my knees up to my chest in order to sit in it, and for a few minutes knew the remembered joy of steaming water around me. The urge to lie down was strong, so I'd raised my legs over the rim – the handle end – sinking back gratefully, splashing water over my chest. I'd stretched my legs and wiggled my toes, and at length set about extracting myself. I couldn't manage it. Somehow I'd become unaccountably wedged. Visions of my inattendance at Midnight Mass assailed me. They would discover me in the morning, goosepimpled and cold, stuck in the tin bath like a turkey ready for the oven. The thought gave impetus to my struggle. After a time I'd managed to stretch my arms back towards the rim of the bed, heaving myself out and laughing at my predicament. It was five years before I took another bath, when bathrooms were installed.

Sister St Richard stayed with me for three weeks. Towards the end of her convalescence, she announced one morning: 'You know, I've never been on a boat.'

'Right,' I said, 'where shall we go?' Expensive, inappropriate cruises flashed through my head. Before I could rally my thoughts, she spoke again.

'What would you say to the Isle of Wight?' she suggested seriously. 'Perhaps we could visit the Abbey at Quarr.'

Sister Mary Francis (Sister St Richard), 1984

I telephoned the ferry company at Portsmouth. The fare for the car and ourselves came within the limit of Sister St Richard's allowance, and four days before her return to the community we set off in the early July morning. Negotiating the car-ferry we eventually emerged at Fishbourne, and I turned the car on to the road that led to Quarr. Built on the site of a much older monastery, this morning the abbey was bathed in sunlight. The bricks of the distinctive bell tower glowed almost apricot. I parked the car and we entered the abbey church, dark after the sunshine, incense pervading the shadows from an earlier Mass. The silence seemed tangible, the sanctuary becoming discernible as we accustomed ourselves to the muted light. I forgot I no longer wore the habit, Sister St Richard kneeling beside me, totally familiar. I would have prolonged the moment, but the Abbot had come from the cloister to greet us. I had known him many years. I introduced Sister St Richard and after cursory formalities he conducted us on a tour of the church and sanctuary, a privilege not usually extended to female visitors. We spoke quietly, appreciative of the Abbot's kindness, and when finally we had come to the end, he escorted us to the car, waving us off with his particular warmth and courtesy. I wished we could have stayed longer. As we turned out of the drive the abbey clock chimed the three-quarter hour.

We took the road to Seaview. The sun was high and the sandwiches we ate by the sea were good. I'd made them before we left – cream cheese, salad and chutney – and we finished them off with bananas and coffee from the thermos. Sister St Richard produced a chocolate wafer bar from her green satchel. The sea air invigorated us and we walked a little before reluctantly turning back to the car. I wished we might have returned to Quarr for Vespers, to have listened once more to the famous Solesmes plainchant, but I knew we must not miss our ferry.

By the time we reached home we were tired. The ferry – the 'boat' – had fulfilled a dream, the mill-pond Solent imparted no physical strain. Coloured sails of small yachts, spread wide like butterflies, lent an ephemeral quality. We both slept happily that night. Sister St Richard's shingles, too, had almost taken their departure.

'Thank you, darling,' she smiled as I delivered her back to the convent two days later, rucksack, bucket and bin liners intact. 'I've loved every minute and feel so much better – and I'll look out some more plants for your garden as soon as I can. Could you do with some honey?'

Washing sheets and towels, cleaning the bedroom again, I smiled at the way the cottage was being used. 'Here I am –' I quoted to myself yet again from Psalm 40 in the breviary: 'How I love to do your will, O God . . .' It was true.

Mary and Anthony, by now established in their refurbished house, were a constant support. I always looked forward to their regular arrivals from Scotland, inevitably accompanied by a flotilla of small dogs. Mark and Julie had acquired two energetic border collies, whose watchfulness was a source of protection should one be needed. As months and seasons tipped into another year, my happiness must have been apparent. I saw swifts return to their nests in the eaves towards the end of May, and grew accustomed to their wheeling swoops and ascents, their exultant cries a background to the summer. When winter came the white hoar frost turned our exposed hillside into a fairyland of beauty. The garden eventually took shape, Sister

St Richard's herbaceous clumps and cuttings proliferated, and each time I visited the convent I came home with further offerings. Friends were generous too, and Mary and I together chose shrub roses to mark the boundaries of my plot. Before long, white wistaria, clematis montana and a climbing New Dawn rose graced the flint cottage wall, and with Pete's help I laid old paving stones for a path, with helianthemums – rock-roses – of every shade to border it. I'd spotted the helianthemum seedlings being sold for a few pence as I drove through a country lane one day.

A friend, visiting for the first time, was enchanted. 'It's anyone's dream cottage –' she mused. I knew what she meant.

Chapter 15

MARCELLE, WHOM I HAD MET when living in the house Stanley lent me in Hove, telephoned one evening. She had written several novels since her book *Nuns* which I had read in the convent. Now, she told me, one of them, *Body and Soul*, was to be made into a film for television. 'But we need a religious adviser,' she explained, 'on location. I thought of you at once.'

'Why a religious adviser?' I asked.

'The novel tells the story of an enclosed nun who comes from her convent for family reasons, and eventually falls in love.' She went on to outline the story. 'Do you think you might obtain permission? They need someone to ensure that the enclosed convent scenes are correct. It would entail your staying in Leeds for about three weeks – do think about it!' she finished.

I asked Sister St Richard and mentioned it to the Bishop's representative for religious in the diocese. They saw no reason why I shouldn't accept. I also met the Bishop himself as he came from a service in the cathedral. He smiled, almost giggled. 'Why not!' he grinned. 'Be an apostle! You can take God's love anywhere!'

I rang Marcelle. 'What's the next step?' I enquired.

I took the train to London where I was to meet Moira Armstrong, the director of the film. She came from Aberdeen, and I liked her immediately. She made coffee, grinding the beans and percolating it as she told me her plans so far. Apart from the details, foreign to me, but which I tried to take in, I kept associating her with mountains – the Cairngorms perhaps, or the long ascent of the Lairig Ghru. It was many months later that I learned of her love of these. She had belonged to a mountaineering group at university.

'We're very lucky,' she said, as we drank the very good coffee. 'We managed to secure Dorothy Tutin to play the Mother Superior, and – a newcomer to us – a very beautiful young actress, Kristin Scott Thomas, for the lead.' She outlined other details of the location and said I would hear from the film's production company.

Too late now for hesitation, and not a little bemused, I made my way home. I received typed particulars from the production office and was booked into the Queen's Hotel, Leeds, for 3 September. Mary and Anthony would be away for six weeks, but Julie next door promised to keep an eye on the cottage. I climbed the small step-ladder in the kitchen and pushed up the loft hatch to extract the suitcase I'd stored there. It was new. I'd found it in a sale and it had small wheels for pulling along platforms. Deciding on clothes to pack was a problem. I rang Marcelle.

'Denim,' she stated. 'Shirts, sweaters and comfortable shoes – oh, and perhaps one tidy thing in case there's a party.' This wasn't too difficult, though I hoped the 'tidy thing' needn't be glamorous. The day before I set off I made two large bags of vanilla fudge – the cast might need sustaining, I thought.

I travelled by train to Leeds.

The hotel was modern and had over seven hundred rooms. I was given room 716. I had not stayed in a hotel for years – and never in one containing seven hundred rooms. I was more alarmed by the matter of ordering food, and tipping, than of meeting the production team. As I crossed the foyer, one of the cast who had overheard my name at the desk, introduced herself. Her name was Olive and she was to play one of the nuns. She and I ate dinner together, discussing the film and the psalm-tones she would be expected to learn, laughing as I tried to sing them to her over the poached salmon. Before we returned to our rooms, one of the assistant directors notified us that we should be picked up by car at 8.30 the following morning.

My room – and the bed – were larger than I could begin to imagine, and the array of towels and soaps and shampoos in the attached bathroom made me long to share them with the community.

Moira Armstrong awaited us downstairs the next morning. She intoduced me to Dorothy Tutin. I would have recognised her voice anywhere, though I had missed her rise to stardom. After further introductions and waiting for late arrivals, we were taken to rehearsal rooms and the 'convent' scenes were run through. Kristin Scott Thomas, as the 'star', slender and lovely, arrived soon after we had assembled.

It was obvious that any ideas of nuns' demeanor had been garnered from Hollywood: the 'community' walked in procession with

On the film set for Body and Soul, *1992*

mincing steps, eyes lowered and totally unrecognisable. I spent the morning trying to disillusion them. The bags of fudge came into their own. Everyone relaxed, and I had amusing conversations between scenes. Elizabeth Bennett told me about her son, then aged eight, whom she had left in the care of a friend. She would telephone him each evening when we returned exhausted to the hotel. The cast were issued with grey habits and black scapulas, which made them happily unrecognisable as any particular Order. The wardrobe mistress asked where she might obtain more kerchiefs – the white head-covering the nuns wore – by Monday. I suggested a local enclosed community, before being cornered by the second director about a book to be read aloud in the refectory scene. I had brought Abbot Marmion's *Union with God* in my suitcase and presented this. Reading aloud to the community at mealtimes had been one of my tasks. I did so every evening, when we were allowed a lighter book. Often the bell for the end of the meal would ring just as we reached a critical moment. Would Mr Darcy return, or was he gone forever? In the current situation *Union with God*, I thought, might be more in keeping.

Long days on location fused into a tapestry of being on hand, advising, and listening, the paraphernalia of filming, so new to me, so familiar to the cast. 'Let's play ping-pong!' Dorothy urged me one morning as we awaited the shooting of her scene.

We unearthed two ancient table-tennis bats from somewhere, and with them a cracked but just usable ping-pong ball, and made do with a rickety table for our game.

'I was table-tennis champion in the convent!' I giggled, recalling our tournaments on recreation days, our circumstances almost as makeshift as now.

We had time for two games and won a game each. 'OK, Playmate,' I laughed, and from then on she would always refer to herself as 'Playmate'. She was to spend many a two-day respite with me later at the cottage. Our evenings would pass with a bottle of her favourite red wine, reading Rilke after a walk to the river as dusk came down, the hills turning misty and blue. She wanted to find a cottage for holidays in Sussex, and I took her to view several properties, sadly without success.

One afternoon on the set the cameraman tapped me on the shoulder. 'Time for you to go up in the cherry-picker!' he grinned. I seemed by now to be regarded as a mascot by the crew. The 'cherry-picker', a huge hydraulic lift, was used to carry spotlights high above whatever needed illuminating. Appalled at the prospect of such a height, I was hard-pressed not to decline, but felt it ill became me to refuse. The cameraman introduced me to the mechanic in charge. I was helped on to the platform, the mechanic joining me before starting the engine. Very slowly we ascended, up and up, until the arm of the cherry-picker was fully extended and almost vertical. 'Hundred and three feet high,' the mechanic informed me. The view was, indeed, impressive. We towered over the roof and surrounding parkland. I was thankful for the rail attached to the platform. I preferred to look ahead rather than down. At last we gradually descended, the mechanic shaking my hand as we disembarked, and I thanked him for the unsolicited thrill. I ran up the steps to the waiting cast. 'I've just been a hundred and three feet up in the cherry-picker!' I shouted boastfully. The hush that greeted me was more impressive than the view. As I turned into the wide hall, I ran straight into a scene being filmed, sound rolling. The teasing from the cast came later.

The day before I was due to leave, Moira Armstrong approached me as Liz Bennett and I stood by the catering van, breakfasting on

Which one is the real nun? The cast of Body and Soul, *Kirklees, Yorkshire, 1992*

bowls of porridge and hot coffee. The morning was damp and foggy, and Moira was deflated. 'I need sunshine for the shooting of the graveyard scene,' she lamented. Rashly, I promised to pray. 'Have you heard the weather forecast?' she replied, the question tinged with sarcasm. I walked down the steps of the terrace, trying to focus my mind. I wished I could get to Mass. I glanced at my watch. It was eight-fifteen. Mass would be celebrated at eight-thirty in the community. I asked to borrow the second director's mobile phone and dialled the convent number. Sister Angela answered and I explained the request for sunshine. Used to my urgent requests, Sister Angela promised to pray. 'By eleven!' I urged, just before she replaced the receiver.

It was just after eleven when work began on the graveyard scene. It involved a procession, and I was called upon to ensure the correct chanting of psalms, as well as the swinging of the incense thurible. The 'priest', too, must look authentic. Moira called for the procession to move. As the cameras began rolling, a shaft of sunlight appeared from what had seemed impenetrable cloud. It touched the grey cloaks of the processing 'nuns', pattening their folds with dappled shadows.

It was difficult not to smile. The morning remained bright for the entire sequence, and I sent a donation to Sister Angela, asking her to buy doughnuts for the whole community. The following evening, after a long day on the set, we found the producer and assistants waiting for us in the bar. They ordered me gin and tonic – I was becoming accustomed to this sophisticated life – and I could see that some kind of presentation was imminent. 'We want to thank you,' the producer said, handing me two framed photographs of the entire cast and crew. I remembered these being taken a few days before, when I was seated beside Kristin and all the other 'nuns', I being the only figure not wearing a habit. A large greeting card accompanied the photographs, the inside completely covered with signatures and messages from everyone. I was overcome. In expressing her own gratitude, the producer had written beneath her signature: 'Please leave your hot-line to YOU KNOW WHO!' I bought a new bed for the cottage with the fee I received on location.

Chapter 16

ACH JULY A CONCERT WAS HELD in the tiny church down the lane. Following this concert, the audience was invited to picnic in the lovely adjoining farm garden, and the annual event became quite celebrated. Anna, who organised the music, asked if she might bring her elderly cousin to tea beforehand. 'Shelagh is nearly ninety,' Anna told me, 'and I feel she might like a rest after her journey from Petersfield.'

Shelagh, elegant, charming, looked twenty years younger. A committed musician, she had studied in Brussels and the Royal College of Music. Today she was brought to the cottage by her god-daughter, Catharine. I made cucumber sandwiches and iced a sponge cake. In due course we made our way to the church and, after Schubert and Mozart, enjoyed our picnic sitting on the collapsible chairs I'd brought, watching the sun go down behind the hill. Conversation was animated but formal, and we promised to keep in touch as I saw them back to Catharine's car, the sky now faded to deep shell-pink. 'I'd like to buy you a house for your antiquity,' announced Shelagh, when I spent a day with her in Petersfield some twelve months later.

I had been in the cottage almost ten years.

'Of course not,' I smiled. I had never taken Mary and Anthony's generosity for granted, but I equally had no wish to become beholden to Shelagh. Returning home, I pushed away the idea despite a strange sense of a continuing saga.

I rang Sister St Richard. 'We'll pray to the Holy Spirit,' she promised.

A few weeks later, I saw Shelagh again. Once more she returned to the subject. I felt the gears were engaging in spite of myself. She was nearing the age of ninety-one, living alone. Her husband, an older widower whom she had married in her late forties, had long since died. An elder brother also had recently died. There were no children to care for her. A residential home was a possibility, but Shelagh was in no way diminished mentally.

Sister Giles at North Stoke, 1994

'If you'll share the house with me, I'll consider it!' I found myself saying. 'I could keep an eye on you – and might just feel I had come half way to earning it,' I finished with some condescension.

Clear as a bell came the words within: 'Here we go again.' Mary and Anthony were incredulous when I tried to explain what was happening. Their generosity had provided an unimaginably blessed cottage, enabling my roots to become established, and from which I would always benefit. It took a considerable time before they were convinced of my sanity in taking on Shelagh. It was an example of their goodness that our friendship was never in jeopardy.

We found a house in a nearby village, newly built in what had been the playground of the village school. We installed a stairlift for Shelagh and arranged for removal men. Ambrose and Monica, typically, had died within a short time of one another a few years earlier – I had given the address at Ambrose's funeral – and I sorely missed their supervision of my move. I hoped they were keeping a spiritual eye on proceedings.

Shelagh insisted on buying the house in my name, with the proviso that should I predecease her it would return to her. I arranged to move from the cottage on 12 December. This time a proper removal van was required, although belongings which had been ample in the cottage now seemed sparse for the house. With Shelagh's own move arranged for 31 December, I knew that the place would soon be fully furnished. The three intervening weeks seemed fraught with plumbers and technicians who each wanted my attention instantly. I remembered Saint Francis and his dislike of ownership. Up until now I had only ever been provided for in faith as each day came; now I supposed I was being taught another lesson. A prayer to the Holy Spirit, already said daily, seemed relevant: 'Tell me what I ought to do, and command me to do it. I promise to submit to everything that you ask of me, and to accept all that you allow to happen to me. Just show me what is your will . . .'

Perhaps I needed to learn about stewardship: to hold without clutching . . . I felt as if my tethering rope had been unhitched. Christmas came, and I joined the community for Midnight Mass, a blessed oasis. Driving back from the convent, stars were bright in a clear sky. I opened the front door of the new house and lit a candle before the tiny crib I'd erected. I remembered a poem, read years before, written by Constantine Tripanos:

Tell me, can this unsuspecting infant staring
At the steep green sky,
be 'He who trampled upon death'?
Everything around him is so poor and so untrue,
The brown ponies like shabby toys, the shepherds stilted
Upon crooks, the Magi wooden kings that dare not bend,
Even the angels, village angels – they could never
Reach the sky again with those flat, clumsy wings.
Silently, unawares and unbelievably come all
Great things: the inroad of great love, the mist of death.

The huge van containing Shelagh's furniture pulled up within ten minutes of her own arrival. She had been brought by one of her young friends from Petersfield. He deposited her and countless items of hand luggage into my welcoming arms. The brandy I had put out in case of needed resuscitation was declined. It was I who could have done with the brandy. Box after box was deposited by the removal men, the mountain ever growing, first in the kitchen, then the

A prayer group at North Stoke

garage. Armchairs, dining table, desk and beds, not to mention pictures, were guided to their allotted rooms. Thankfully, she had bequeathed the Bechstein to the Hindhead School of Music, her fingers no longer able to play her beloved Schubert or Brahms. We snatched soup and sandwiches sitting marooned at what was visible of the kitchen table. Shelagh's resistance was steely. Her aunts had not been prominent in the suffragette movement for nothing. 'I can't believe we've made it!' she beamed. At last the removal men, determined to finish in time to celebrate New Year's Eve, departed. Dirty tea mugs were piled in the kitchen sink.

'Don't let's do any more today,' I pleaded, fearing for her survival.

I had made up my spare bed for Shelagh, planning to exchange it for her own in the morning. We used everything already unpacked from the cottage and ate vegetable lasagne and mince pies on the now slightly more cleared kitchen table. This time there was no hesitation over the small glass of whisky beforehand. I helped Shelagh to bed and prayed she would negotiate any need for the bathroom during the night. We had a bathroom each, very small, but perfectly adequate. I wished her goodnight and made certain the landing light was left on.

We slept fitfully, but thankfully. The New Year slipped in unheralded after the whisky and I came down in the morning to find Shelagh virtually upside down among the cartons of books. 'Wait till I've fixed the bookshelves!' I scolded. I unearthed the hand-drill from the garage, fitting rawl-plugs into the holes I'd drilled. 'All yours,' I teased her as she started sorting the titles.

For both of us there was much to discover. We had come to know each other over the months, but this was a case of living together, joined at the hip, so to speak. We had agreed, indeed insisted, on separate telephone lines, mercifully as it turned out. Shelagh's appetite for telephone calls was considerable. Typically she would not hear of my contributing to council-tax or other domestic bills. I was adamant I should contribute in ways that I could, and took on all cooking and household chores. In jest I would sing 'I can't give you anything but LERVE, Baby!' which became a much quoted refrain.

Friends telephoned, concerned for both of us. 'She'll never survive,' said one of them, 'you can't make a move like this at ninety-one.' Another, retired from nursing, confided, 'She'll fall, you know. The hip will go and that will be the finish.'

They did not know Shelagh. We remained together, in that house, for almost seven years, happier with each day. Shelagh maintained her links with friends, attending concerts and listening to music on her stereo. Father Francis once more blessed the house, as he had blessed the cottage. We instituted Mass again and each month this took place in the dining room. Shelagh, a devout Anglican, nevertheless loved to attend, and enjoyed meeting everyone who came. After a few weeks we had sorted and re-arranged most of the furniture, and daily commitments gradually resumed, just as they had at the cottage. The car, a Honda, bought from a legacy left by an aunt the previous year, at last found a space in the garage.

We had been in the house three weeks when Mrs Gray, whose house was opposite ours in the little square, caught me one day as I stood considering what to do about the completely unmade garden.

'I know you pray for people, Sister,' she stated as she walked across to me. 'Would you be able to pray about the house we are hoping to buy? This one is too small for us, but we need permission for the agricultural place we want, and this is very difficult to obtain.' I promised to do my best, but was rather dubious about getting round agricultural permits, even with prayer.

Dorothy Tutin in my sitting room, 1995

A month later, Dorothy – she had become 'Dottie' by now, came to stay for two nights. She was free from a long stint in the theatre and wished to visit Sussex again. She also wanted to inspect Shelagh and the new house. On the Tuesday morning, Mrs Gray came across again. 'Oh THANK you, dear Sister,' she beamed, 'the permission has come through, and we are putting this place on the market now.'

I grabbed Dottie. 'Do you want that house opposite?' I giggled.

Dottie's reaction was immediate. 'May I see inside?' she enquired.

'Of course!' responded Mrs Gray. 'Come and look over it now, if you'd like to.'

So Dottie bought a cottage, within a stone's throw of us.

Chapter 17

THAT CHRISTMAS DOTTIE'S LEUKAEMIA was diagnosed. 'The consultant says I have choice. Either strong chemotherapy which may kill me, or a much less severe treatment from which I just might survive longer,' she told me on the telephone. 'I don't know which to decide.'

An arrow of sadness hit me. 'You'll have to discuss it with Derek,' I answered, from a sudden numbness inside. 'And Nicky and Amanda, of course.'

Dottie's daughter Amanda had recently bought a house quite near us. She was pregnant. Ben, her baby, was to become Dottie's first grandson in the July. Nicky, like all the family, was in the theatre.

Dottie, typically, chose the stronger chemotherapy.

'Pray for me, Playmate,' she said. Derek brought her down to their cottage after her first session of treatment in hospital. She had spoken to me from the hospital several times, but I was unprepared for the shock of her drawn face when she walked across to us. She and I sat in the summerhouse, a burst of early spring sunshine giving a touch of unexpected warmth. I knew that the scarf she wore over her hair was to hide the lack of it. Dottie's faith had never been conventional. 'Give me some healing,' she would ask me as the year sped on. I prayed with her as I could, and daily when she returned for yet further sessions in hospital. Amanda, too, produced endless homeopathic remedies.

The treatment, with periods off for respite, continued through to the end of the year. Hopes were raised, then dashed. Ben's birth was a landmark of joy. In the New Year's Honours list Dottie was created a Dame. The award ceremony was postponed in the hope of her being able to attend later. When at last she could get to the Palace, Derek, Amanda and Nicky supported her, a star performance from them all. She wore a specially designed turban over her wig. Just at that time a surprise *This is Your Life* programme was televised. As ever, the trouper in Dottie rose to the occasion, and only a few could imagine the severity of her illness. I was invited to take part, and sat with many a stage personality on the set. At the party afterwards Dottie came across to hug me.

'Darling!' she beamed. 'I need a drink! I never guessed! And to think that you're here too!'

I explained that the BBC had sent a car and – more to the point – was conveying me home too. It was almost three in the morning before I crept into the house. Catharine, Shelagh's god-daughter, had arranged to stay the night, but we waited till breakfast to have a full account of the televised excitements.

'Come and watch tennis with me,' Dottie telephoned from the cottage. It was Wimbledon fortnight and she had the television in her room. I curled up beside her on the large bed, trying to concentrate on the tennis. Derek, attentive as ever, produced strawberries. The tennis reached a climax. The stress, as always, was unbearable. I glanced at Dottie. She had fallen asleep.

'I wish I had your God-magic,' she said one day. She was spending most of the time at their cottage now, the London house too far away. I wished I had more myself. Not magic, but faith. Nicky had married Sophie in the May, Amanda's Ben was now one year old. Derek, with the prospect of Dottie's loss, reminded me of Basil at The Hollies. By the end of July Dottie was admitted to the Macmillan Unit at Midhurst. No more chemotherapy.

I took my turn sitting beside her in the bright hospice room. Mostly there were no words, at others a moment of clarity emerged. I prayed as I had prayed beside Elizabeth, a midwife again. The community had long since been asked to remember Dottie. I knew that they were. The last time I saw her she had just woken. Her mind, clouded by the palliative medicine she was receiving, seemed momentarily alert. She clasped my hand. 'Oh, it's YOU,' she beamed, 'I don't BELIEVE it.' I squeezed her hand, but she had fallen into a coma again. Her death came very early on 6 August.

That morning, still in bed, I read my breviary for the morning office before going to wake Shelagh. The homily for the feast of the Transfiguration, 6 August, was from a sermon by St Anastasius of Sinai:

Since each of us has God within him, and is transformed into his divine image, let us cry out with joy: 'it is good for us to be here.' For here all is light, and joy, and happiness and bliss, here is the heart at rest, in peace, serene.

'That is my prayer for you, dearest Dottie', I whispered.

Shelagh, now ninety-six, was becoming more frail. Not in her mind, but physically. Walks were confined to the garden, with the aid of the walking-frame. We still made expeditions in the car, but these were less adventurous. Her sight became impaired. Recorded music was her constant consolation, and so were her many friends. Christmas came, and on Boxing Day she went down with a cold, staying in bed for a few days. The cold, as it had often done, went to her chest, but this time seemed reluctant to respond to treatment. I called the doctor, who prescribed antibiotics. They, too, had little effect. 'I think I'm going to die,' she informed me, without emotion. The doctor came again. 'Please don't try to get me well,' she told him. A wise man, he said we should let nature take its course.

Shelagh grew rapidly more weak. I would have been glad to have had a break from people dying, but I knew that some day with Shelagh this must come. The six years since we bought the house had been far more blessed than I had dared hope. I knew an ending one day was inevitable.

Her ninety-seventh birthday loomed. We bought a helium balloon inscribed with 'happy ninety-seventh birthday' and secured it to her bed-table. Many friends sent flowers, and Catharine and her husband Patrick came with champagne. When the Vicar arrived to bring her Communion I heard her tell him: 'I've made it! I've outlived any member of my family!'

A few days later, as I sponged her face after breakfast, she became serious. 'I think the time has come to look for a home,' she said. 'We always said that we would do that if I became bedridden – I think this is the moment.'

In my heart I knew it too. I was very tired. Lifting her to the commode I had strained a muscle in my arm. It had become very painful. 'I hate to let you down,' I began.

'Nonsense!' she reprimanded. 'These years have been the happiest in my life . . .'

It was I, of course, who had benefited. I began searching for a suitable home. Vastly expensive and never particularly appealing, at last I found one that I thought might just possibly be suitable. Shelagh, practical now, seemed adapted to the prospect. The telephone rang that evening. A friend from Hampshire wanted to know if I'd found a home for Shelagh.

'Well – nearly,' I told her.

'I meant to ring you yesterday,' she continued, 'I have a young friend whose mother-in-law is beautifully cared for in a residential home near Chichester. It is called Lordington Park. The mother-in-law is ninety-one – would you like Lizzie's telephone number?'

'Oh yes!' I was emphatic down the telephone.

Lizzie and her husband Henry lived near the residential home.

I rang her up. 'Come over tomorrow, if you'd like that,' she invited me. 'I'm seeing my mother-in-law and could take you with me, so that you could inspect the place.'

The following morning, 27 May, I attended Mass. I wanted to pray for whatever lay ahead. I stood with the rest of the congregation as the priest walked to the altar. He wore red vestments. 'Today we are remembering Blessed Margaret Pole,' he announced. 'She was martyred at the Tower of London on 27 May 1541. She was the Countess of Salisbury in her own right, and was given in marriage to

Shelagh on her 95th birthday

Sir Reginald Pole. They lived near Chichester, at Lordington Park . . .'

I thought my ears were deceiving me. Lordington Park. I was astonished. That very afternoon I was to inspect the place for Shelagh. 'Blessed Margaret Pole,' I earnestly begged, 'over to you!'

I met Lizzie at 2 o'clock and we drove the short distance to Lordington. The gabled flint house was visible from the road; it stood in parkland, on rising ground, obviously designed to catch the sun. Lawns ran down to a ha-ha; in surrounding paddocks horses grazed, peacefully unconcerned. We saw the stables as we turned up the drive. Several dogs of unspecified breeds lay in the sunshine as we drew up to the house.

'Here we are,' said Lizzie.

We were admitted by one of the staff. She smiled and greeted Lizzie, who introduced me. 'All right to go up?' asked Lizzie.

The entrance hall, plain-carpeted, led to an elegant staircase. I noticed a chair-lift had been attached. An alcove displayed a lovely arrangement of flowers. Later I would be shown the large drawing room, a few wing chairs placed before tall windows, and low tables within easy reach. French doors led to a terrace overlooking the grounds. Immediately noticeable was the grand piano, a Blüthner. No need, I knew, to look further.

As Lizzie led me upstairs my immediate impression was of a quiet order. There were no untoward smells, no plastic buckets. Lizzie took me to meet her mother-in-law, whose stroke had left her immobile and without speech. I held her hand a moment as Lizzie busied herself about the room. Mrs Rutland looked in.

'Mrs Rutland, this is Sister Giles,' said Lizzie. 'Is there a chance you have a moment to spare?' Mrs Rutland owned and ran the residential home. She had remarkably lovely eyes. I followed her down to the office, and told her about Shelagh. We discussed fees. I knew I had found the right place for her. Mrs Rutland wrote down all Shelagh's particulars.

'I'm sure you would love Shelagh,' I assured her. 'She's a musician,' I added, as if that were an asset.

Mrs Rutland's face lit up. 'I love music,' she told me. 'In fact,' she confided, 'I am taking piano lessons – even at my age!'

'We do have a waiting-list,' she went on. 'Usually a long one, but there is just a chance of a room becoming vacant in about three weeks. Would you like me to let you know?'

Not a second's hesitation withheld me. 'Oh, please,' I said. (BLESSED Margaret Pole, I added silently to myself.)

On 21 June the St John's Ambulance men transferred Shelagh to Lordington Park. Catharine travelled with her in the ambulance and I followed in the car with her belongings. Frail, but totally alert, she is eagerly awaiting her hundredth birthday.

We are planning a concert in the drawing-room.

The End

THE TRAIN DREW AWAY FROM THE STATION. It was uncrowded. I'd found a window seat without difficulty. I'd been asked to conduct a retreat in a country house in Northumberland, giving talks to invited guests and sharing a few extra days with my hosts. It was March, the winds still cold, but daffodils had opened in spring sunshine, yellow drifts flanking the long drive to the house. The retreat finished, Wanda had taken me in the car to the Lammermuir Hills. We'd eaten home-baked rolls and cheese and apples near a farmhouse beside the climbing road, before reaching Nunraw, the Cistercian monastery isolated high on the hills, in time for Vespers. Kneeling in the bare chapel I'd thought again of Thomas Merton, whose writings had meant so much to me. I'd quoted him in one of my retreat talks:

> God's image is in us all, and we
> discover him by discovery
> of the likeness of his image in one another.

Another day we'd visited Lindisfarne – Holy Island – crossing the long causeway when the tide was low, curlews and oyster-catchers picking their way on spindle legs through the sandy shallows beside us. Lindisfarne was redolent with Celtic spirituality, of St Columba and the monks from Iona who had come there in the seventh century. We stopped to talk to a shaggy island pony, eyeing us over the gate. He looked windblown and sturdy, as if he were as old as the island itself. Tonight though I should sleep in my own bed. There would be Shelagh to see tomorrow, letters to answer. I thought of this with a sense of remoteness. Even in so short a time I'd felt an affinity with the wide landscapes of the North. As the train gathered speed the woman opposite worked at a crossword. Pen in hand, she looked up as we drew into Newcastle, but quickly resumed her concentration. She wore her pink cardigan tightly buttoned. I wondered where she lived. Travelling brought together diverse companions, years later a face or gesture awoke memories of a forgotten journey.

I can only say there we have been; but I cannot say where.
And I cannot say how long, for that is to place it in time.

Eliot's lines matched the movement of the train as well as my introspection. A ticket collector came through from the further compartment, steadying himself against the outside seat as he clipped my ticket. Curly grey hair escaped from his ill-fitting cap. 'I'm going through to Sussex,' I explained, fearing the destination on my ticket might seem unfamiliar. 'Well, even I've been to Brighton!' he smiled, before moving down the carriage.

I picked up a newspaper I'd bought at the station. Headlines looked dismally normal. I laid it on the table in front of me, then decided to find the buffet. These days I was brave. I swayed the length of three carriages and paid for my coffee without a qualm.

Next week I should visit the community. They'd be interested to hear of Lindisfarne and Nunraw. I would tell them of Wanda's ridgeback hound, looking so fierce but unexpectedly gentle when known. With Fred no longer alive, everyone missed a dog in the community.

We were drawing near London now. Stations flashed by in closer sequence, our speed still too great to read names. Factories and warehouses spilled alongside the track, hoardings took over from trees. I reached for my anorak, bundled beside me on the seat. 'We are approaching King's Cross,' I heard over the speaker. 'Please make sure you have all your luggage with you when you leave the train.' Reaching the end of a journey was an anachronism. I'd long ago discovered it was only the beginning of another. I recalled setting out for The Hollies, then returning from Devon with Peter, in faith following wherever the road had led. Now I must cross London, haul my belongings on to another train at Victoria. Ultimately there was only ever one journey. Boethius, writing in the fifth century, had caught the gist of it. Luckily his medieval Latin had been translated by Helen Waddell:

> To see Thee is the end and the beginning
> Thou carriest us, and Thou dost go before,
> Thou art the journey, and the journey's end.

I waited for the doors of the train to open. Two youths ahead of me still played their personal stereos. The crossword woman, paper tidied away, smiled as she reached for her case.